Blockchain Lingo

By Edwin Ongola

Blockchain Lingo

A tool for self-certifying your Blockchain literacy

ISBN (paperback): 978-9914-779-31-8
ISBN (e-book): 978-9914-779-33-2

Layout and cover design by Edwin S. Ongola

Front cover photo by OpenArt AI/ChatGPT as prompted by Edwin S. Ongola (quality enhancements by Simon Mwakio – Tel: +254721490466 email: seymourmwakio@gmail.com)

Note: No other section of this book has been produced with the aid of any AI Tools

Back cover photo by Emmanuel Odera Ongola

Publisher: Edwin S. Ongola
blockchainlingo25@gmail.com

Printed in the US & Kenya.
December 2025: First Edition

Reviews

This is the ultimate guide to start off your blockchain journey. The author demystifies the subject with personalized ease and clarity, making the book suitable for both scholars and industry users at any level. Chapter by chapter, chapter into chapter, the flow of content allows the reader to immerse, learn, and self-test at their own pace.

I, without a doubt, highly recommend it to anyone looking to become an expert in blockchain. This book is a must-have for sound self-certification.

Linda Ongola-Oyieke

Table of Contents

List of Abbreviations

API	Applications Programming Interface
ASICs	Application Specific Integrated Circuits
BCT	Block Chain Technology
BPA	Business Process Automation
CBDC	Central Bank Digital Currency
CeDeFi	Centralized-Decentralized Finance
CEX	Centralized Exchanges
CIA	Confidentiality Integrity Availability
CIAAA	Confidentiality Integrity Availability Authenticity Accountability
CKMS	Cryptographic Key Management System
CPUs	Central Processing Units
DEX	Decentralized Exchanges
DIDs	Decentralized Identifiers
DKMS	Decentralized Key Management System
DPKI	Decentralized Public Key Infrastructure
DAO	Decentralized Autonomous Organizations
DLT	Distributed Ledger Technology
DoS	Denial of Service
ERC	Ethereum Request for Comments
EVM	Ethereum Virtual Machine
GDPR	General Data Protection Regulation
GPUs	Graphics Processing Units
ICO	Initial Coin Offering
IDO	Initial Dex Offering
IoT	Internet of Things
M2M	Machine to Machine
NFT	Non Fungible Token
OOP	Object Oriented Programming
P2P	Peer to Peer

PDS	Personal Data Store
PKI	Public Key Infrastructure
RSA	Rivest Shamir Adleman
SaaS	Software as a Service
SCF	Standard Contract Form
SDS	Secure Data Stores
SCO	Security Coin Offering
SHA	Secure Hashing Algorithm
SPoF	Single Point of Failure
SSI	Self-Sovereign Identity
TTP	Trusted Third Party
URIs	Uniform Resource Identifiers
VC	Verifiable credential
VDR	Verifiable Data Registry
VP	Verifiable Presentation
ZKP	Zero Knowledge Proof

Acknowledgements

My first acknowledgement goes to George Kinyua, my former high school classmate. A couple of years ago, George and I would have long phone calls, exploring business ideas. On one of these calls, when I told him that I was writing a paper for peer review, he insisted that I should write a book – any book. George would later make follow up calls to find out what progress I had made regarding the book. Well, finally almost two years later, the book is ready. Hopefully, it is the first of many. Thank you, George Kinyua for your encouragement.

Secondly, I would like to acknowledge the large number of individuals behind the sources listed in the reference sections, located at the end of each chapter of this book. Collectively, your input is invaluable.

Thirdly, to my sister Linda Ongola-Oyieke. She is our family "misungu", a mother, a wife, and an author. Yet she has always spared some of her precious time to proof read my writings, including this one. Linda, thank you for your feedback. I owe you.

Fourth, to Dr. Jacob Magero of Kenyatta University, who is a former colleague and a friend. Thank you for accepting to read my manuscript. As a serious academic, I know you would have read it, albeit at your convenience, even if Kenyan lecturers weren't on strike. In addition, thank you for your feedback and for accepting to write the foreword for this book.

Finally, I would like to acknowledge my mum together with my sisters, Brenda and Ada. Whereas they were unaware that I was writing this book, the gaps they filled from time to time indirectly contributed to this project's success. Thank you very much.

Foreword

Technology has been an indispensable aspect that has, since time immemorial, been the basis for the propulsion of human life to the ever increasing efficiency, convenience, effectiveness and comfort for man. Through an evolutionary process, Information Communication Technology (ICT) in particular, has ultimately relatively revolutionized the social, economic, political, and religious spheres of human life. Through the Internet, there has been a drastic change and improvement in human life, relative to, say thirty years ago. In light of the primordial openness of the Human mind, notwithstanding the finitude and fallibility of the same, technology (and more specifically ICT) offers even much greater prospects for making human life even more livable in terms of efficiency, effectiveness, convenience and comfort, notwithstanding the attendant and co-occurring ethical and moral issues and concerns . Currently, the concept of Artificial Intelligence (AI) is in a sense a dominant topic in discourses in academics, science, technology and mathematics, with the cognate moral and ethical overtones and implications. The focus of this book, its strength and competence, does not however rest in the Philosophical dimensions arising from or attendant to Technology as such or ICT in specific but rather the very foundational, academic and educational rubric and practical import of ICT and specifically blockchain technology.

The book fundamentally targets those who are interested in blockchain applications such as cryptocurrency, employment of blockchain technology in business, or just seeking to keep abreast with the latest developments and knowledge in ICT. The book is quite expository, explicative and concise to the extent that it is highly relevant and so, a "must read" for those who intend to delve in the academic and professional realms and dimensions of Information Communication Technology. The philosophy that informs the entire body, essence, goal and purpose of this book is the postulation that with the ever expanding technological knowledge and the complexity and bounds of Information communication Technology, no academic or commercial undertaking should tolerate or accommodate doubtful judgments of amateurs but only encourage, accommodate and enhance those who are better informed about the methods, techniques and applications in Information Communication Technology.

In this book, there is a presupposition of no necessary training in the field of ICT for its readers as such. This is because blockchain technology is increasingly attracting people with backgrounds outside of the ICT space. The book is quite self-contained with regard to the notion of blockchain technology and this is evidenced in the wide coverage of relevant topics from what a blockchain is, the history of blockchain, why blockchain? The benefits of blockchain technology, areas of application, blockchain concepts, just to mention but a few. For purposes of illustrations, subtle nuances are exposed, numerous examples are given, figures and diagrams are also provided. There are as well exercises, quizzes, and answers to the same, just to jog the mind of the reader after every topic.

The book appears in ten Topics/Chapters all quite well laid out and bountifully topical. It provides an extensive survey, overview and thereby constitutes a very concise but comprehensive exposition and explication of blockchain technology. In light of blockchain technology, what has been provided is "the true north", a verisimilitude to academic and intellectual acumen and achievement on one side and a demonstration of how theory can be put to test through technology with actual, real-life value and significance. To the preceding extent, the author "has the wind in his sails" towards educating and informing his readers. What has been provided by the author is a repository of knowledge and information with regard to blockchain technology. The work is an outstanding academic contribution to the realm of Information Communication Technology (ICT) with enormous practical import and immeasurable cognitive and ontological significance and value. The book is highly recommended as a companion text for any student taking a course in Information Communication Technology (ICT). The book can be summed up as something that looks like the future but also talks to the past.

DR. JACOB MAGERO

(Lecturer in Philosophy, Kenyatta University, Kenya)

Cover Illustration

The scene on the cover of *Blockchain Lingo* depicts a group of people who seem to be conversing with each other in a blockchain themed garden. However, judging from the speech bubbles, they are each speaking a different language from the others. Therefore, they are not actually conversing with each other, but to any individual from any community in the world, who might lay eyes on the front cover of *Blockchain Lingo.*

Starting with the man in shorts, and moving in a clockwise direction, the direct translation & meaning of the content of each speech bubble, is as follows:

The first man asks, "Do you speak blockchain?" What he is asking is whether the reader understands blockchain technology. He targets the English speaking people of the world.

After him is an Indian man who says " मैंने पहले ही ईथर का उपयोग करके पुरी खरीद ली है ", to mean "I already bought puri using Ether". Puri is an Indian dish and Ether is a cryptocurrency. This is an "Indianish" way of saying "Of course I know what blockchain is. In fact I am already using it". Needless to say, he targets the numerous Hindi speaking citizens of the world.

Next is the lady who says "¿Es bitcoin?" in Spanish to mean "Is it bitcoin ?". This speech is important because it associates bitcoin which is well known to blockchain technology. She targets parts of Europe and South America.

Then comes the Arab man, who represents the Middle East and parts of Africa. He says "بـ عض لـ دي NFTs" to mean "I have some NFTs", thus acknowledging familiarity with blockchain technology and inviting his target audience to find out what NFTs are.

After him is the lady seated on the bench, who says in French, "Tu veux dire comme les cryptos ?" which translates to, "You mean like cryptos ?". This also links cryptocurrencies to Blockchain Technology. Her audience is in Europe, Canada and parts of West Africa.

Last, is the African woman, who asks "Sio mpesa ?" in Swahili. This translates to "It's not mpesa ?" thus inviting the curious to contrast between MPESA and cryptocurrencies. MPESA is the dominant Mobile Money Payment/Transfer application used around East Africa. Her target is the Swahili speaking communities in that region.

Together, the six people are saying that there are many aspects to Blockchain Technology and it is relevant to everyone. So everyone is invited to read *Blockchain Lingo.*

Preface

Why the book?

Whereas blockchain technology has been with us for over a decade now, it is increasingly attracting people of various cadres outside the ICT field. Some want to invest in blockchain applications like cryptocurrency, others may want to employ it in their business and others still, just want to keep up with their knowledge in ICT developments. The latter group may include ICT professionals who barely have the time to go through scattered, voluminous materials, in order to get a concise, but informative picture of this new field.

This book is intended to be a one stop shop for introductory information about blockchain and some of its applications. Current buzzwords like blockchain, bitcoin, cryptocurrency, smart contracts, NFTs, and others are explained in manner that allows one to gain a firm understanding of concepts in the field. Hopefully, on completion of this book, the readers will have the confidence to engage in constructive conversations about blockchain and possibly desire to get more knowledge in order to work with it in a productive manner.

"Those who love wisdom must investigate many things"
– Heraclitus

Who should read this book ?

This book is written for the average Joe, which we all are, outside our fields of expertise. Therefore the book is suitable for teachers, management, ICT professionals and any other group of individuals, including school going children who have an interest in the field.

How to contact us:

Email: blockchainlingo25@gmail.com

Facebook: https://web.facebook.com/blockchainlingo

Dedications

To Grace. They call you "Messi" but I call you "My D". When you came looking for me in the rain, I knew you loved me and that you cared. Thank you.

To Emmanuel. I want to continue calling you my "Sonny boy", but I see and respect that you are fast growing into a man. Fortunately, you are "Mountain" too. So, become a mountain - actualize your full potential. Thank you for the bottle of Coca Cola you bring along for me whenever schools close.

To May. Thank you for your long standing, selfless, and unwavering support. Few people - probably no one else would match a quarter of your sacrifice. God bless you abundantly.

1. Introduction

"The outrageous is reasonable if introduced politely"
- Charles Fort

1.1 Why Blockchain

To manage storage and retrieval of data, we use databases. Many different types of databases exist and they can be classified according to use case, deployment, data model, and storage method. For example, classification based on data model includes Hierarchical, Network, Relational, Object-oriented and NoSQL databases. Classifications based on deployment could be whether it is centralized, decentralized or distributed. Deployment classification could also be whether it is local or on the cloud. Blockchain technology falls in the decentralized category. Ultimately, the choice made regarding a database system affects scalability, performance, integrity, storage space, and data privacy. It is therefore important to have an appreciation of database system types and products so as to make the right decisions to meet project requirements[1].

In a situation where a database is shared by many remote users, we consider the system to be centralized. In such a case, there is likely to be a central administrator who manages access control of the database. This administrator has to be trustworthy since he has complete access to the entire database. One problem with this setup is that, it may be possible to make alterations to the data without leaving a trace. Secondly, it portends a single point of failure in the sense that the system is susceptible to a denial of service (DoS) attack or other situations that can render the host inaccessible. Whereas one could argue that a distributed database could solve the latter problem, it should be considered that the distributed system could still be under a single administration or company, which implies that the system is still amenable to manipulation. It is these kinds of problems that blockchain technology attempts to solve.

1.2 A History of the Web

You have probably heard of the term "web 3.0" being mentioned. The number 3.0 just points to the version of the internet based on how it is (or was) used.

In the first version of the internet (web 1.0), it was primarily used for dissemination of information. The content was mostly static text with occasional simple graphics. The user participated as a consumer of encyclopedia-like content created by major institutions such as universities, media companies and a few tech savvy individuals.

Come the early 2000s, and the internet evolved into an information sharing, collaborative and networking tool. Users no longer just consumed other people's content, but they could contribute to information on platforms like wikis and could also easily create their own content using blogs. It was in this era that many social media platforms like Facebook (now Meta) sprang up enabling the creation of online communities based on shared interests. Video and photo sharing also became common place with platforms like YouTube and social applications like WhatsApp. This period is dubbed "web 2.0".

The problem with web 1.0 & 2.0 is that, institutions rather than the common internet user, controls most platforms. For example, these platforms control what their members can post and in some extreme cases, can close an individual's account without affording them the opportunity for recourse. Then there is the problem of surveillance capitalism. These institutions are in a position to programmatically monitor activities of members and can sell what they glean about their members to advertising companies and research organizations, without the knowledge and permission of the subjects of the data.

With so many institutions and even governments now offering diverse online services, users have had to maintain many accounts and passwords. Other than this, so much of their data is held by so many entities and yet the users have no control on what is done with it. They may with time, even forget who is in possession of their private data.

Web 3.0's genesis is actually Bitcoin network, the first successful mechanism by which people can transfer value and data directly, peer to peer, securely, without reliance on a Trusted Third Party (TTP). It is for this reason that Web 3.0 is also referred to as the "internet of value". Web 3.0 is an attempt to democratize the internet in such a manner that individuals have as much chance as corporate organizations to control and benefit from some online social and economic activities. The technology enabling web 3.0 is blockchain[2].

After the successful implementation of blockchain technology for bitcoin cryptocurrency, not only did other cryptocurrencies begin to emerge, but other non-fintech use cases also started cropping up, especially after blockchain systems themselves, evolved from being special purpose like Bitcoin, to general purpose like Ethereum[3]. What was the attraction?

1.3 Benefits of Blockchain Technology

As far back as 2018, in testament to the promise of blockchain technology, PwC surveyed 600 executives in 15 countries and territories. Of these, about 84% reported that they had blockchain initiatives underway, while about 15% claimed to have fully live blockchain systems[4]. Shortly after in 2020, in its annual Global Blockchain Survey, Deloitte interviewed 1,488 senior executives across 14 countries and about 55% of respondents said that blockchain was critical and in their top-five strategic priorities[5].

The attraction to blockchain technology has largely been due to four key properties, which I cover briefly below:

1) Consensus: The participating nodes (computer systems) have a programmatic way of coming to an agreement on which valid transactions should be stored next on the shared ledger, such that, ultimately, all nodes have the same records.
2) Finality: After transactions are committed by consensus, they cannot be rolled back.
3) Immutability: You cannot delete, or edit, without detection, any transaction, once it is committed on the blockchain.
4) Provenance: As a result of the first three, there is a complete history of all transactions ever recorded on the blockchain.

A few additional benefits exist. These are:

- Transparency: Except where a "privacy blockchain" is involved, generally speaking, all transactions can be viewed using an appropriate software tool designed for that purpose.
- Security: Asymmetric cryptography and hashing is used to ensure authenticity, integrity and non-repudiation. Non-repudiation means that a sender cannot later deny performing a transaction signed by him (i.e. using his signature).

- Smart contracts: These are basically codified agreements or operations, to be carried out automatically without human intervention, under certain predefined circumstances.

Subsequent chapters of this book will delve a little deeper on these benefits[6].

A more recent study by Demand Sage reported that, by 2025, there were 560 million people worldwide who use blockchain technology. Asia topped the list with 160 million people. They also reported that by 2024, there were 617 million cryptocurrency users worldwide and 10,025 cryptocurrencies that were actually active. Of the businesses surveyed, 90% reported deploying blockchain technology in some capacity. Demand Sage further predicts that the blockchain market will reach $162.84 billion by the year 2027[7].

1.4 Areas of Application

Early blockchain technology implementations were designed to benefit the general society. However, the business sector soon realized that the technology had the potential to streamlines business processes and make them more efficient, accountable and secure. Moreover, the cost savings blockchain promised could not be ignored. Consequently, two broad categories of blockchain applications have emerged.

Among the business community, it was the finance sector who took interest first, because of the threat that cryptocurrencies posed to them. Banks for example, are the expensive middlemen that cryptocurrencies are intended to eliminate. Then the supply chain industry quickly realized that blockchain's properties of immutability, transparency and security was naturally suited for provenance tracking[8]. Many more industries are now either exploring or actually employing blockchain in their businesses. Research by CoinLaw in 2025, reports that 83% of the people who they surveyed, said they are "very confident about using blockchain technology to streamline financial reporting and transparency"[9].

Governments can use blockchain technology to streamline processes in various departments, and also to become transparent and accountable in many of its activities. For example, elections results can be made more transparent if blockchain technology is employed. Governments can also use blockchain for Identity management.

Industry	Market Share (%)
Banking and Finance	30
Government	13
Insurance	12
Healthcare	8
Media, Entertainment & Gaming	8
Generic	6
Technology Services	6
Professional Services	4
Energy & Utilities	3
Others	7

Table 1.1 Distribution of Blockchain market share by industry[10]

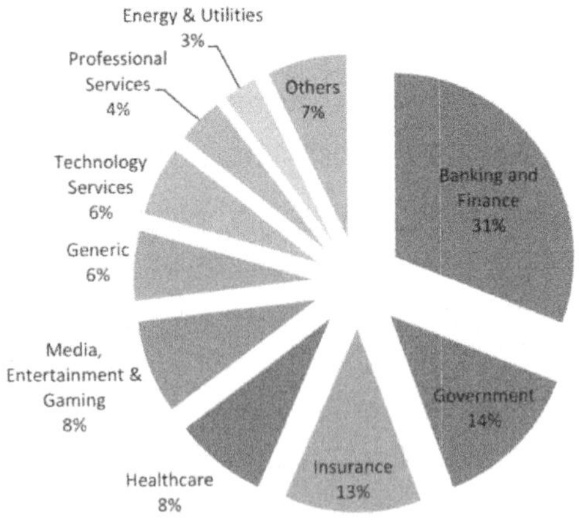

In healthcare, other than providing conditions for great efficiency, blockchain technology can be used to facilitate secure sharing of patient data. Blockchain data can also be a dependable source for medical research because of its integrity[11].

Using smart contracts to automate policy issuance, claims verification, and payouts, the insurance industry can become more efficient in terms of time and money. Blockchain technology can help them realize cost savings due to reduction in fraud, paperwork and number of employees[12].

One of the key benefits that blockchain technologies bring to the Media and Entertainment industry is disintermediation. Creators are enabled to interact directly with their customers or fans. Using smart contracts and Non Fungible Tokens, counterfeits can be reduced, and royalty payments can be directed straight to creators. All these result in more favorable income for the artists[13].

The energy sector has been shifting towards a decentralized model where independent producers using solar panels, wind, or hydro turbines are able to sell excess power to the main grid or directly to their neighbors. Blockchain technology can be used to track production, consumption and payments for this type of energy ecosystem[14, 15].

Another sector where blockchain technology is useful is Education. Here, it can be used for record keeping and also for verification of credentials.

The list of sectors covered in the above paragraphs is not exhaustive, because just like other technologies, blockchain itself is also still evolving and therefore its use cases are growing by the day. Perhaps by the time you finish reading this book, you will have found a new way of using blockchain gainfully in your field(s) of interest.

1.5 The Roadmap Ahead

In the rest of this book, different basic aspects of blockchain technology will be covered to strengthen your foundational knowledge of the same.

The next chapter (second), is about **Blockchain Concepts**. Here, you will come across the data structure underlying the technology. From this, you will get a better appreciation concerning the benefits alluded to earlier in this chapter.

Since blockchain technology is heavily dependent on cryptography, the third chapter, **Cryptography Simplified**, covers some basic terminology and concepts relevant for some of the chapters ahead, and probably the rest of your quest for knowledge in the computer science/security domain.

Blockchain technology is ultimately just a decentralized storage structure. So the fourth chapter, which is on **Decentralized Apps**, briefly covers deployment alternatives for you to gain clarity on blockchain infrastructure. Subsequently, the interaction mechanism with the data structure is also described.

For most business exploring or employing blockchain, the single most draw is probably smart contracts. It is what enables automation and if done properly, results in business efficiencies and cost savings in a multitude of ways. So the fifth chapter is on **Smart Contracts**.

Payment (transfer of value) remains the largest use case of blockchain technology. It is likely that even projects initially not connected to, or intended for payment, will eventually incorporate aspects of payment in them. After all, isn't it cryptocurrencies that announced blockchain technology to the world? So chapter six is on **Cryptocurrencies**.

If you pay attention to business news, then you will probably have heard of "tokenization". Chapter seven covers tokens, drawing attention to the different types. You will also understand why chapter seven's heading is **Non Fungible Tokens** and not just tokens.

From the inception of the internet, users have been identified through an authentication process where they submit some type of user name and password. Apart from the constant security risk of impersonation, such login credentials are cumbersome to maintain over multiple online platforms. So chapter eight is on **Self-Sovereign Identity**, an authentication mechanism that gives power over identities back to the owners. In case you are wondering - of course, it is related to blockchain.

Blockchain technology is not a silver bullet for all businesses or industries. So in chapter nine, a process that one could use to establish **Suitability of Blockchain** for a given business is covered.

Finally, chapter ten covers a small subset of **Current & Future Trends**.

Conclusion

There are several reasons as to why blockchain technology literacy is important. For one, it is currently like the internet in 1990s, which has since become so common place, that even those who cannot define it know how to use it, because they require it for one reason or another.

With many governments talking up Central Bank Digital Currencies, people will have to learn how to operate a crypto wallet or at least, familiarize with the dangers of such government controlled systems. That aside, it is cheaper, especially for cross border payments, to use crypto rather than the traditional methods.

Since many businesses are likely to take advantage of blockchains' promises of reduced risk, lower cost, and better customer experience, it follows then that, they will be seeking knowledgeable and skilled workers for implementation and maintenance of their systems. At the moment there are still many opportunities for entrepreneurs, software developers and project managers in Blockchain industry.

For CEOs who do not wish to look bewildered as they are spoken to like children by younger IT staff, basic domain knowledge is a must, not just to save face, but for decision making as well.

Exercise 1

1. Do a brief research on **Relational** databases and summarize your findings in space provided below.

2. Briefly research on **NoSQL** databases and summarize your findings in spaces provided below.

3. List any five web 2.0 applications that are not mentioned in this chapter.

   i. ________________________________

   ii. ________________________________

   iii. ________________________________

   iv. ________________________________

   v. ________________________________

Quiz 1

1 Fill in the blanks.

Databases can be classified according to use case, ___________, data model, and storage methods.

a) centralized
b) relational
c) no SQL
d) deployment

2 Which of the following **best describes** web 3.0?

a) It is the internet of value.
b) It has blockchain networks such as bitcoin and users have control over their own data.
c) It is an evolution stage of the internet that is characterized by decentralization, artificial intelligence, token-based economics and users have control over their own data.
d) It is the internet of identities.

3 Which of the following statements is **true**?

a) Provenance is made possible due to finality and immutability of blockchain transactions.
b) Finality and immutability have the exact same meaning.
c) Provenance tracking and auditing have no relation to each other.
d) The consensus mechanism requires users to vote before each transaction is committed onto the blockchain.

4 Which of the following statements are **false**? (you may choose one or more)

i. Asymmetric cryptography and hashing is used to ensure transparency.
ii. Non-repudiation means that a receiver cannot later deny receiving a transaction.

iii. All blockchain systems are transparent.
iv. Provenance means that only the most recent records are available for scrutiny.

a) ii only
b) ii and iv only
c) i, iii and iv only
d) All of the above

5 Complete the statement.
The supply chain industry primarily uses blockchain for ______________________.

a) streamlining financial reporting
b) provenance tracking
c) redundancy
d) identity management

6 Which of the following sectors is **least likely** to be attracted to blockchain due to its identity management benefits?

a) Education
b) Supply chain
c) Medical
d) Government

7 Complete the statement.
In the media and entertainment industry, blockchain technology enables creators to interact directly with their customers or fans, primarily due to ______________________.

a) redundancy
b) provenance
c) disintermediation
d) immutability

8 Which of the following statements is **false**?

a) Using smart contracts and NFTs, counterfeiting of digital products can be reduced in media and entertainment industry.

b) In the banking and finance industry, blockchain technology can help by streamlining financial reporting and providing transparency.
c) There is no use case for blockchain in the energy and utilities sector.
d) Blockchain data can be a dependable source for medical research.

9 Which of the following statements are **true**? (you may choose one or more)

i. The government can use blockchain technology to ensure accuracy and transparency in voting processes.
ii. Blockchain technology can be used to track consumption and payments in a decentralized energy production ecosystem.
iii. The only use case for blockchain technology in the education sector is identity management.
iv. The insurance industry can use blockchain technology to automate policy issuance, claims verification, and payouts.

a) i only
b) iii only
c) ii, iii and iv
d) i, ii and iv

10 Fill in the blanks.

In the education sector, blockchain technology can be useful for ________________ and ____________________ among other things.

a) record keeping, verification of credentials
b) claims verification, payouts
c) record keeping, claims verification
d) disintermediation, finality

References:

1 GeeksforGeeks (2020). *Types of Databases.* [online] GeeksforGeeks. Available at: https://www.geeksforgeeks.org/dbms/types-of-databases/ [Accessed 22 Sep. 2025].

2 Lacity, M.C. and Lupien, S.C. (2022). *Blockchain Fundamentals for Web 3.0.* University of Arkansas Press, pp.38, 47-48.

3 Infante, R. (2019). *Building Ethereum Dapps: Decentralized Applications on the Ethereum Blockchain.* Manning Incorporated, p.205.

4 PricewaterhouseCoopers (2018). *PwC study shows four out of five executives (84%) surveyed report blockchain initiatives underway.* [online] PwC. Available at: https://www.pwc.com/jm/en/press-room/blockchain-initiatives.html [Accessed 23 Sep. 2025].

5 Ledger Insights (2020). *CFTC chair encourages principles-based approach to regulating digital assets - Ledger Insights - blockchain for enterprise.* [online] Ledger Insights - blockchain for enterprise. Available at: https://www.ledgerinsights.com/cftc-chair-encourages-principles-based-approach-to-regulating-digital-assets/ [Accessed 23 Sep. 2025].

6 Bradley, M., Gorman, D., Lucas, M. and Golby-Kirk, M. (2019). *Getting Started with Enterprise Blockchain: A Guide to Design and Development.* 1st ed. USA: O'Reilly, pp.18-19.

7 Kumar, N. (2025). *Blockchain Statistics (2025) — Adoption Rates & More.* [online] demandsage. Available at: https://www.demandsage.com/blockchain-statistics/ [Accessed 23 Sep. 2025].

8 Bradley, M., Gorman, D., Lucas, M. and Golby-Kirk, M. (2019). *Getting Started with Enterprise Blockchain: A Guide to Design and Development.* 1st ed. USA: O'Reilly, pp.70-71.

9 Elad, B. (2025). *Blockchain Statistics 2025: Key Trends, Growth Metrics, and Industry Insights.* [online] CoinLaw. Available at:

https://coinlaw.io/blockchain-statistics/ [Accessed 23 Sep. 2025].

10 D'Souza, J. (2025). *Blockchain Statistics By Market Size, Revenue, Demographics, Benefits and Facts.* [online] Electro IQ. Available at: https://electroiq.com/stats/blockchain-statistics/ [Accessed 24 Sep. 2025].

11 Ashurst, S. and Tempesta, S. (2022). *Blockchain applied : practical technology and use cases of enterprise blockchain for the real world.* Boca Raton, Florida: Routledge, pp.138, 152.

12 Tymoshchenko, D. (2024). *8 Blockchain Use Cases in Key Industries | 2024 Guide.* [online] Acropolium.com. Available at: https://acropolium.com/blog/use-cases-for-blockchain-technology-adoption-across-major-industries/ [Accessed 24 Sep. 2025].

13 Protokol (2020). *Top 5 Blockchain Use Cases in Media and Entertainment.* [online] Protokol. Available at: https://www.protokol.com/insights/top-5-blockchain-use-cases-in-media-and-entertainment/ [Accessed 24 Sep. 2025].

14 Cohen, A. (2024). The Blockchain Revolution In The Energy Market. *Forbes.* [online] 6 Dec. Available at: https://www.forbes.com/sites/arielcohen/2024/12/06/the-blockchain-revolution-in-the-energy-market/ [Accessed 24 Sep. 2025].

15 Inetum (2021). *Blockchain is shaping the future of energy infrastructure services.* [online] Inetum. Available at: https://www.inetum.com/en/blockchain-shaping-future-energy-infrastructure-services-0 [Accessed 24 Sep. 2025].

2. Blockchain Concepts

"You can never really get away from the fundamentals of anything that you're doing"

- Amari Cooper

2.1 Introduction

This chapter describes what block chain is in general and the basic concepts about it.

Blockchain is a type of Distributed Ledger Technology (DLT), which is a data structure that resides across multiple computing devices[1] that may not necessarily belong to the same individual or organization. Blockchain can be used to track and share information about anything deemed valuable such medical records, shipment tracking details, land titles and financial records, just to mention but a few.

2.2 Basic Structure

As a ledger, blockchain stores records or transactions in chronological order, which are lumped together once some threshold is reached, into a data structure called a block. If it is the first block in the blockchain, it is known as a genesis block[2]. A block has two main sections as depicted in figure 2.1. One is for storing transaction data, and the other for storing data about the block. The latter is known as the header section.

Generally speaking, a block stores in its header section, the timestamp for when the block was created, a hash of the previous block and a Merkle Root Hash. Some blockchain implementations may store more information in its header, but for the purpose of our current discussion, these three should suffice.

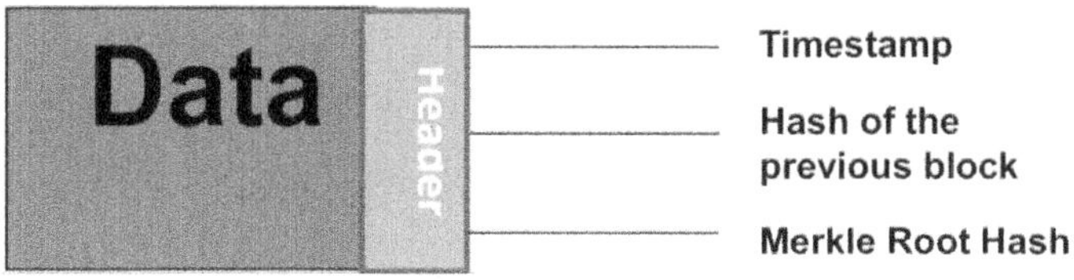

Figure 2.1 Basic Block Structure

2.3 Data Integrity

Now, a hash is like a seal. Its primary use is for detecting alterations on data. To generate a hash, an input is fed into a hashing algorithm, which produces an output of a fixed length, irrespective of the size of the input. For example, if you feed any input into the hashing function called SHA256, it will always generate an output of 64 characters. So if you feed the word "**h**ello" into the SHA256 algorithm, the output will be:

2cf24dba5fb0a30e26e83b2ac5b9e29e1b161e5c1fa7425e73043362938b9824

If we change the input to "**H**ello", with the first character, h, now capitalized, the SHA256 algorithm will give us:

185f8db32271fe25f561a6fc938b2e264306ec304eda518007d1764826381969

As can be seen from the above, a slight change in the input, even to a single character, would result in a completely different hash from the previous one. So if a hash of a block is computed and stored in the block during creation, it is later possible to re-compute the block's hash in order to compare with the stored hash value. If the hashes do not match then the block contents have been tampered with.

Note that different hashing algorithms may produce different outputs for similar inputs and different blockchain developers may opt for alternative hashing algorithms.

A Merkle root hash is a hash of the data or more specifically the transactions in the block. Its name stems from Merkle Tree "a data structure that holds hashes of data, then hashes of those child hashes, then hashes of those parent hashes, and so forth" [3].

As an example, consider a block that stores just a total of just 4 transactions as depicted in figure 2.2. Each of these individual transactions would be hashed individually to produce hash1, hash2, hash3, and hash4. From the resulting 4 hashes, a new hash would be computed from hash1 and hash2 to produce hash12. Yet another one will be computed from hash3 and hash4 to produce hash34. Finally, a new hash which represents all four transactions is computed from hash12 and hash34 to produce hash1234.

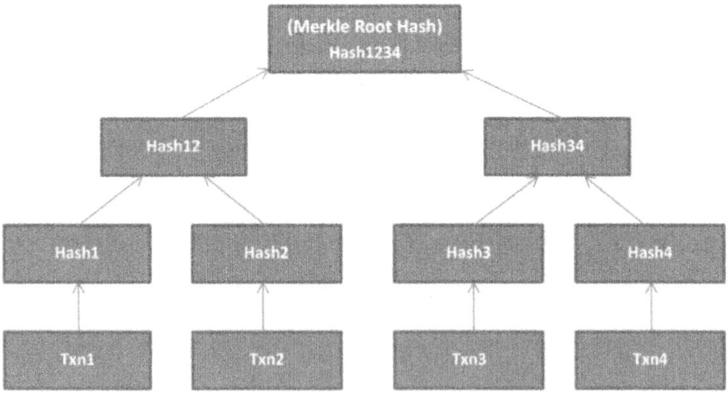

Figure 2.2 Merkle Tree Structure

Our example only considers 4 transactions. Suppose each block stored hundreds of transactions, the Merkle root hash would still have to be constructed in a similar fashion. The computational overhead required to construct it would be much higher. Clearly, the cost of making an alteration in any of the transactions once a block has been created and confirmed is prohibitive. This is why blockchains are considered tamper resistant.

2.4 Chaining Mechanism

At this point, the concept of a block should be clear however, where the "chain" part comes in, is yet to be addressed. After all, it is common to see blockchain represented by images like figure 2.3:

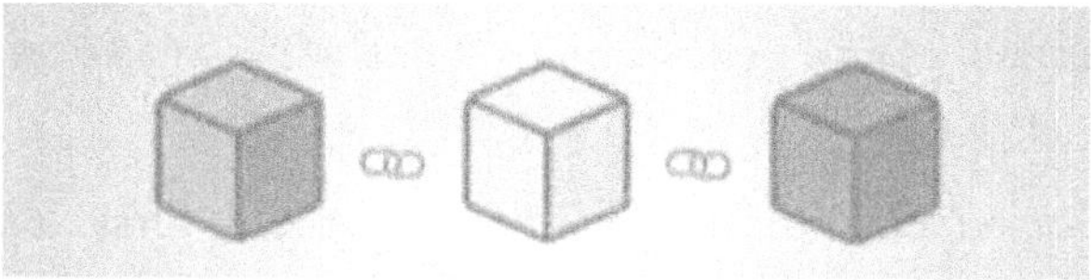

Figure 2.3 Depiction of a blockchain system[4]

Well, as earlier mentioned, a block also stores the hash of the immediate prior block in its header section. So block 2 stores the genesis block's hash, Block 3 stores Block 2's hash, Block 4 stores Block 3's hash and so on. It is these hashes of previous blocks, stored in subsequent blocks that form imaginary chains, tying blocks in chronological order[5].

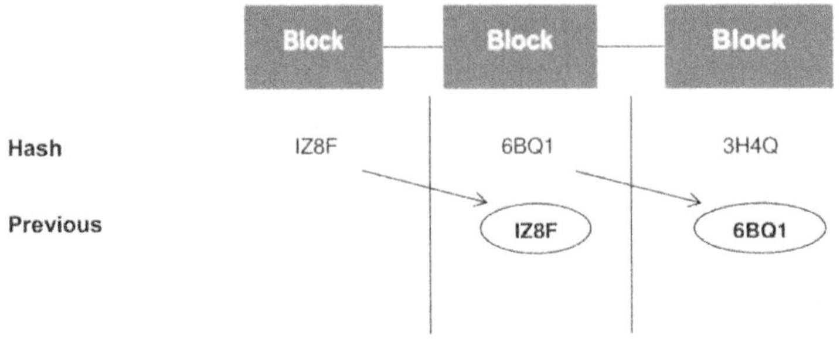

Figure 2.4 Conceptual chaining of blocks

The implication of this chaining of blocks using hashes is that, a change in an older block would require that the hashes of all subsequent blocks be recalculated and updated. For example, if there were ten blocks and a slight change is made on the genesis block, then the hash of the genesis block will have to be recomputed and stored afresh within the block and then be updated on block 2. Block 2's hash would also have to be recomputed and updated on both Block 2 and Block 3, because of the update of the genesis block's hash. This will continue on until Block 10.

So in blockchain, a hash plays two key roles. First, it uniquely represents the contents of a block and secondly it is used for chaining blocks in chronological order[6].

Recall that a blockchain is replicated on many computers. If an attempt is made to edit a blockchain on a given device, these changes have to be replicated to other hosts as well. As this happens, the edited chain is likely to be ignored by most of the other hosts, due to consensus mechanism, which are algorithms that coordinate the inclusion of new and valid blocks onto a chain. Nevertheless, the important point is that a blockchain data structure is very difficult to tamper with without attracting attention. Therefore, most applications using blockchain technology employ it as an "append-only" structure i.e. data written on it, is not intended to be edited nor deleted.

The term used to reference specific blocks on a chain is "block height". This refers to the number of confirmed blocks before the specific block of interest. So, for a blockchain currently with 20 confirmed blocks, the block height for the last block is 19. To view block information including the Block height, a tool called "block explorer" is used[7].

2.5 Types of Blockchain Networks

From the definition of a blockchain network, it should be clear that the system lends itself to an environment where a computer network exists and there is a need to share data. There are 3 different types of blockchain network implementations.

The first one is a public blockchain or permission-less blockchain. In this case, any entity may join the blockchain network, without permission and unilaterally elect to participate in any of the capacities made available to the public. The entity can also choose to quit the network at any point without consultation. Data stored on public blockchain should generally be open to scrutiny by the public and social actors rely on built-in mechanisms i.e. algorithms to assure trustworthiness of the data[8]. Examples of public blockchains include cryptocurrency networks like Bitcoin and Ethereum.

The second possibility is a private blockchain or a permissioned blockchain. Here some sort of administrator must exist to authorize and grant new users with access rights and to revoke them whenever the user is no longer required to participate in the network. So rules and policies have to be designed to manage the addition and removal of new nodes and users into a permissioned blockchain[9]. This scenario would apply to private organizations that seek to keep their data secure, but do not want to lose their autonomy. A good example would be a national organization like a bank or insurance company that has branches across the country.

Finally we have consortium blockchains, which are also private permissioned blockchains. The difference here is that, sections of the blockchain will be under the control of different organizations that have the need to share data. A good example of where this arrangement would work is where government regulatory authorities require access to data from the organizations that they have oversight of. So these organizations would maintain control of their own data while granting permission as is necessary to relevant outside parties like government auditors. The reverse could also be true[10].

2.6 Positive Aspects of Blockchain Networks

What is the allure of blockchain technology? The first beneficial feature is its decentralized nature. This makes it a fault tolerant system since data is available from other nodes should one or some of them become unavailable. Then there is also the fact that the redundant copies are not under one administration and therefore trust is transferred to the systems consensus mechanism. In other words, the actors rely on correct operation of algorithm to ensure authenticity and integrity of the data.

The second benefit is immutability. Because of the computational cost involved in making a block and the encryption requirements, it is difficult and therefore prohibitive even for a well-resourced actor to compromise the integrity of the data stored in a blockchain system. This makes most blockchain implementations "write-only" systems that can't be tampered with or erased.

The third benefit is provenance. This means that with a blockchain system it is possible to get a complete audit trail of all transactions of interest. This is because of the use of time stamps for all records and the blocks that house them. Moreover, encryption mechanisms are employed not just to assure integrity, but to aid in the chronological chaining of blocks.

The fourth benefit is that a blockchain system potentially eliminates the middle-man. This is especially evident with implementations in the financial sector, particularly with cryptocurrencies. Consider a scenario where one wants to make a cross border transfer of cash. An individual would have to go physically to a bank where he or she has to do some foreign exchange and also divulge the purpose of the transfer and the recipient details. Eventually, the transfer would involve the central banks of the two nations and the recipient's bank. The time spent at the bank could take 30min or even two hours depending of many factors. The actual transfer could take three to seven days before the recipient has access to his/her money. Finally, not only will the sender will be changed a tidy percentage of the amount being transferred, but she or he will lose some money from the foreign exchange. Contrast the above scenario with a bitcoin transfer, which can be done online at literally any location of your choosing. Moreover, the recipient should receive their money into their wallet within ten minutes in the exact same currency and with no involvement of a third party. To wrap it up, the transaction cost is miniscule in comparison to what banks charge. Clearly, the elimination of middle-men also results in the benefit of huge reductions in transaction costs as well as time savings as described earlier in this paragraph[11].

Conclusion

In this chapter, blockchain has been presented in a simplified manner. The reader now knows what it is, where it is applicable and what its benefits are. It should therefore be easier to delve deeper into the subject using more advanced texts.

The next chapter covers cryptography. Blockchain technology uses it to ensure data authenticity, integrity and auditability.

Exercise 2

1. What is a blockchain fork? Mention the types of blockchain forks that exist.

2. Describe consensus mechanism in blockchain technology.

3. List 5 consensus mechanisms

i. ______________________________

ii. ______________________________

iii. ______________________________

iv. ______________________________

v. ______________________________

Quiz 2

1 Which of the following statements is **true**?

a) In a blockchain, the timestamp for when the block was created is stored in the body section of the same block.

b) In a blockchain, the timestamp for when the block was created is stored in the body section of the next block.

c) In a blockchain, the timestamp for when the block was created is stored in the header section of the same block.

d) In a blockchain, the timestamp for when the block was created is stored in the header section of the next block.

2 Which of the following is **not true** regarding blockchain consortia?

a) The nodes on a consortium blockchain network are managed by ordinary members of the public.

b) The nodes on a consortium blockchain network are managed by different companies, but no single company is in charge of the network or the data.

c) Some companies join consortium blockchain networks to accelerate learning and to influence standards.

d) A consortium blockchain network is useful for exploring use cases and building proof of concepts.

3 Complete the following sentence.
The tool used to view block information on a blockchain is called a ______________________.

a) Internet Explorer

b) Blockchain dashboard

c) Blockchain previewer

d) Block Explorer

4 Which of the following statements is a **true description** of a public blockchain?

a) Public blockchains are open to anyone to participate in the mining and validation processes, however to conduct transactions, permission is required.

b) A public blockchain is a permission-less network where any participant can upload data to the ledger and the data can be viewed by anyone.

c) In a public blockchain, users can execute transactions via the network in a peer-to-peer manner, but have to rely on a trusted third party.

d) In a public blockchain, anyone is allowed to upload data to the network, but viewing the ledger is controlled.

5 Complete the following statement.

Censorship resistance is ______________________________

a) another term for an "append only" ledger in a blockchain network.

b) the ability of blockchain network to resist attempts to censor, alter or stop the flow of information.

c) the ability of a decentralized system to make it easier for someone to prevent others from using the system.

d) when transactions can be unjustly blocked, scrutinized, or manipulated by authorities.

6 Which of the following statements are **true**? (you may choose one or more)

i. Blockchain technology's decentralized nature makes it fault tolerant.

ii. Blockchain technology reliance on cryptography makes it immutable.

iii. With blockchain technology, one can get a complete audit trail of transaction concerning a given entity or object

iv. Provenance on a blockchain structure is made possible through cryptography.

a) All of the above.
b) i, ii and iii only
c) i and ii only
d) None of the above

7 Which of the following statements are **false**? (you may choose one or more)

i. Private blockchains are also known as permission-less blockchains.
ii. A hard fork is a release of new software version that alters a blockchain system's functionality in a manner that is not backward compatible.
iii. Most enterprise blockchain solutions are unlikely to be private-permissioned blockchains.
iv. The allure to private-permissioned blockchains is that they provide assurances of resource efficiency, fast settlement times, confidentiality, and regulatory compliance.

a) ii, iii and iv
b) i only
c) i and iii
d) None of the above

8 Which of the following **best describes** the benefits of blockchain networks?

a) Cryptography and tamper resistance.
b) Immutability and hashing.
c) Provenance, immutability and fault tolerance.
d) Chronological ordering of records and provenance.

9 Complete the following statement.
The consensus mechanism used in Bitcoin is ___________.

a) Proof of Stake
b) Proof of Concept
c) Proof of Work
d) None of the above

10 Which of the following statements is **false** about blockchain forks?

a) A blockchain hard fork occurs whenever a blockchain converges into a single unified path.

b) A blockchain hard fork requires all nodes or users who wish to move to the new chain to upgrade to the latest version of the software.

c) When a blockchain fork occurs, it means the nodes in the network are not in agreement regarding the future state of the blockchain. This could be temporary or permanent.

d) A soft fork is a backwards-compatible change to a blockchain's consensus mechanism.

References

1 Hellwig, D., Karlic, G. and Huchzermeier, A. (2021). *BUILD YOUR OWN BLOCKCHAIN : a practical guide to distributed ledger technology*. S.L.: Springer Nature, p.4.

2 Hellwig, D., Karlic, G. and Huchzermeier, A. (2021). *BUILD YOUR OWN BLOCKCHAIN : a practical guide to distributed ledger technology*. S.L.: Springer Nature, p.12.

3 Hardman, D. (2021). SSI architecture: The big picture. In: *SELF-SOVEREIGN IDENTITY : decentralized digital identity and verifiable credentials*. S.L.: O'reilly Media, p.103.

4 BuiltIn (2013). *What Is Blockchain Technology? How Does Blockchain Work? | Built In*. [online] Builtin.com. Available at: https://builtin.com/blockchain [Accessed 27 Apr. 2022].

5 Shen, M., Zhu, L. and Xu, K. (2020). *Blockchain : empowering secure data sharing*. Singapore: Springer Nature, p.15.

6 Ahameda, M. (2020). *Blockchain in data analytics*. Newcastle Upon Tyne: Cambridge Scholars Publishing, p.85.

7 S, A. (2023). *What is Block Height?* [online] BitDegree. Available at: https://www.bitdegree.org/crypto/learn/crypto-terms/what-is-block-height [Accessed 1 Apr. 2025].

8 Lemieux, V.L. and Feng, C. (2021). *Building decentralized trust : multidisciplinary perspectives on the design of blockchains and distributed ledgers*. Cham, Switzerland: Springer, p.140.

9 Lemieux, V.L. and Feng, C. (2021). *Building decentralized trust : multidisciplinary perspectives on the design of blockchains and distributed ledgers*. Cham, Switzerland: Springer, p.99.

10 Ahameda, M. (2020). *Blockchain in data analytics*. Newcastle Upon Tyne: Cambridge Scholars Publishing, pp.5–6.

11 Krishnan, S., Julie, E.G., Robinson, Y.H., Balaji, S., Kumar, R. and Balas, V.E. eds., (2020). *Handbook of Research on Blockchain Technology*. London: Academic Press. p.214.

3. Cryptography Simplified

"In cryptography, we trust the math, not the myth."
- Vitalik Buterin

3.1 Introduction

It is common to come across definitions of blockchain technology that mention cryptography. For example:

> "Blockchain is a growing list of digital records stored in groups, within a data structure called a block, and these blocks are chronologically ordered, and are linked together and secured via cryptographic mechanism"[1].

So, to further understand blockchain and some of its implementations, one is required to have a basic understanding of cryptography. In the second chapter, some aspects of cryptography were touched on, in order to understand the blockchain data structure. The crucial role hashing plays in chaining blocks together, and also in ensuring data integrity, was also explained. In this chapter other important aspects in cryptography are covered without being overly mathematical.

3.2 Fundamentals of Cryptography

Cryptography refers to mechanisms for encrypting and decrypting information. The term originates from the Greek language, and is composed of two words. "kryptós", the first one, means "secret". The second one is "gráphein", and it means "writing". In other words, cryptography involves the conversion of intelligible text or messages, to unintelligible format, in order to assure some aspects of CIAAA security principals. CIAAA is an acronym, and its full form is depicted in figure 3.1[2].

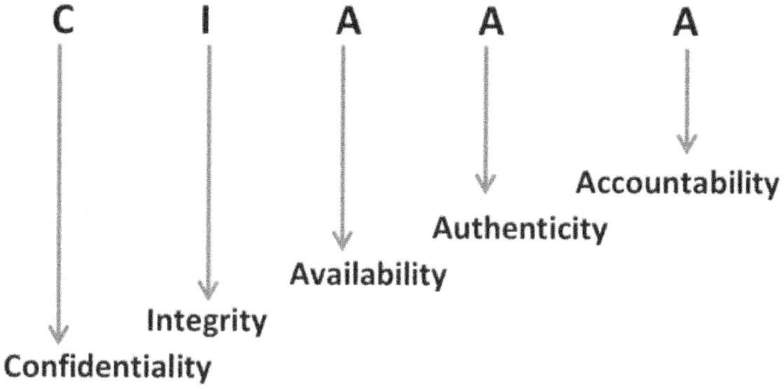

Figure 3.1: CIAAA Security principals

The one who encrypts information is referred to as a **cryptographer**. The one who studies encrypted information, possibly with the intention of decrypting it, is known as a **cryptanalyst**[3].

3.3 Classic Ciphers

Cipher is yet another term for encryption. **Decipher** is the reverse of cipher i.e. to decrypt some information. Whereas the current generation may boast of a wide array of sophisticated tools for encryption and decryption, cryptography as a concept is not entirely new. Our ancestors too had a need to secure information, so that it was not accessible and/or understandable to undesirable elements.

Two methods were commonly used to handle encryption in the days of old. The first one is substitution and the second one is transposition. Both are rather simple.

In the substitution method, each character is replaced with another at the source, and the recipient has to know how to reinstate each of the original letters correctly, in order to make sense of the message. For example, if the sender wants to send a message such as "Ambush at dawn", using the chart in figure 3.2, the transmitted message could read "Codwuj cv fcyp".

A	B	C	D	E	F	G	H	I	J	K	L	M	N	O	P	Q	R	S	T	U	V	W	X	Y	Z
C	D		F				J					O	P					U	V	W		Y			

Figure 3.2: Substitution method of encryption

In the above example, each letter has simply been replaced by the one two places ahead of it. In other words, "A" in position 1, has been replaced by "C" in position 3; "U" at position 21 has been replaced by W in position 23 etc. Predictably, on reception, the receiver ought to know that he/she should substitute each letter, with the one that is two positions in front of it.

There are three problems with the substitution method. The first one is that the encryption/decryption mechanism has to be kept secret. One way of achieving this, is by constantly changing it e.g. from character+2 to character-1.

But how does the sender keep the receiver posted on these changes? Because if a messenger carries both the encrypted message and its decryption method, assuming that the messenger himself is trustworthy, there is the risk of the cipher text being intercepted and easily being deciphered by an adversary. The second issue is that once an entity has known the encryption/decryption method, they could intercept a message, decrypt, modify it, encrypt it again and send it on its way. e.g. "Ambush at dawn **after 2 days**". The third issue is that the simplicity of the encryption method is such that, by repeated guesswork alone, even without a computer, one could infer the actual message from the cipher text.

The transposition method differs from the substitution method in that, instead of replacing letters using some key, characters are swapped by position as depicted in figure 3.3. For example character at position 2 goes to position 5; the one at position 5 goes to position 2, character at 6 to be swapped with the one at 14 etc.

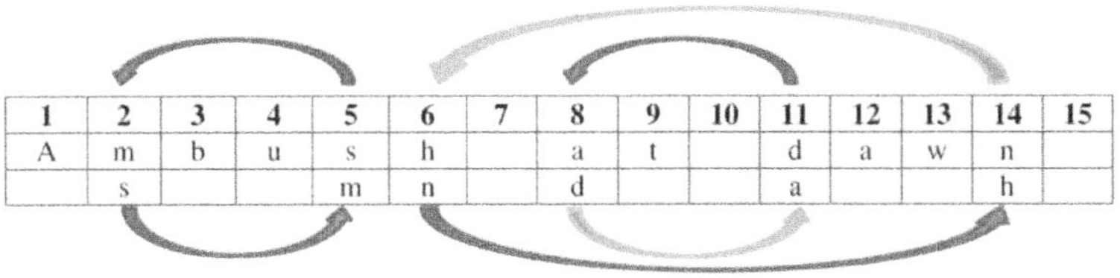

Figure 3.3: Transposition method of encryption

This transposition method, while a bit more complex, will still have two of the same concerns as the substitution method. The first one is how to handle the encryption/decryption mechanism and the second one is the ease with which one could decipher the message without prior knowledge of the method used for encryption.

3.4 Symmetric & Asymmetric Encryption

Modern encryption methods are more sophisticated and can be categorized into two groups, namely symmetric and asymmetric encryption.

In cases where the sender and the receiver use the same key for encryption and decryption, we call this symmetric encryption. In other words, the same password, or passphrase that is used to convert a message into cipher text, is the one used by an inverse function to reverse the process, in order to make the message intelligible to the receiver. Therefore, the receiver must know the key, which brings us back to the concern regarding how to securely transmit the decryption key. Otherwise messages can easily be intercepted, read and perhaps modified before being forwarded to the intended recipient. This is a form of "man in the middle attack". Symmetric encryption is currently not employed in blockchain technology.

Asymmetric encryption on the other hand uses two separate keys, one for encryption and the other for decryption. The receiver need not know the key used for encryption, in order to decrypt the message. Also, unlike in symmetric encryption where the key is supposed to be private for both, the sender and receiver, asymmetric encryption generates two keys, from which only one key is made private. The private key remains with the sender, and the other key, known as a public key, is made accessible to potential communication partners. So the sender encrypts with the private and upon receipt of the cypher text message, the receiver decrypts it using the public key.

It is important to note that these keys work together as a pair in such a manner that, only those with the sender's public key, can decrypt a message encrypted with the sender's private. Other than ensuring confidentiality, this pairing also ensures non-repudiation i.e. the sender cannot later deny having sent a certain message, if it was encrypted with his private, because he alone has this private key. So this also acts as a digital signature for the sender.

Public-private key pairs can also be used to assure confidentiality in the sense that a message encrypted using a public key, can only be decrypted using the associated private key. Therefore, only the owner of the private key, whose public key was used to encrypt a message, can decrypt the message to read it.

A few examples of algorithms used for asymmetric encryption include Elliptic Curve Digital Signature Algorithm (ECDSA); Rivest Shamir Adleman (RSA), which is named after 3 scientists who developed it i.e. Ronald Rivest, Adi Shamir and Leonard Adleman; Diffie- Hellman-Merkle Key Agreement.

The description and individual workings of the above algorithms can extend several pages. However, in this book, details that are not pertinent for the understanding of overall basic concepts of asymmetric cryptography are not covered. Suffice it to say that, blockchain technology is heavily dependent on cryptography, particularly aspects of asymmetric encryption, for successful operation.

3.5 Hashing

Hashing was introduced in the previous chapter to explain the concept of chaining in a blockchain data structure. This section covers a few more terms related to hashing.

As a recap, a hashing function is an algorithm that takes an input of any size and encrypts it to produce an output of a standard size. For example, SHA256, a hashing function, will always generate an output of 64 characters, irrespective of the size of the input. This is depicted in figure 3.4. The output is called a **digest** (or hash value) and the input is called a **pre-image**.

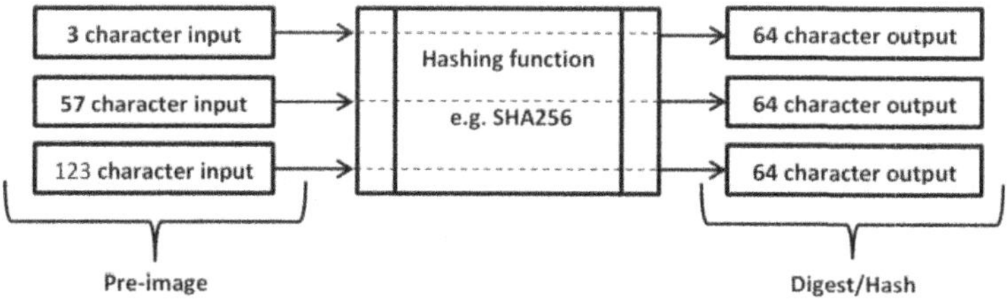

Figure 3.4: A hashing algorithm produces a standard output size

Hashing functions are "one way" functions, meaning that, it is extremely difficult to figure out the pre-image from the digest, even computationally using brute force methods. This is called **pre-image resistance**. To complicate things further, hashing functions are also "many to one" functions, meaning that some pre-images could result in the same digest as depicted in figure 3.5. So in a rare event, where a cryptanalyst manages to recreate a pre-image from a digest, the pre-image would probably be an incorrect one. When two or more pre-images result in the same hash, we call this a **hash collision**.

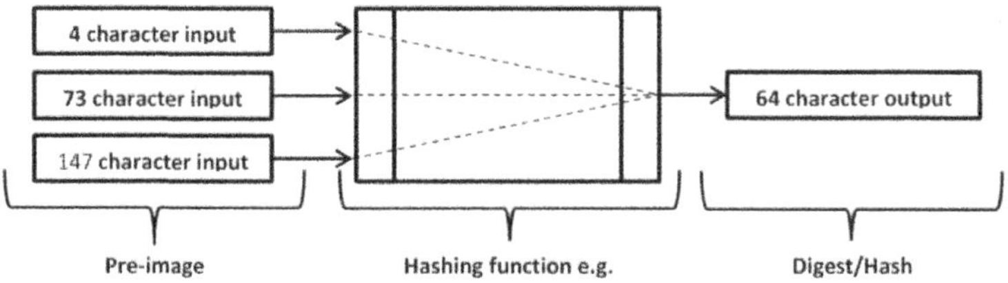

Figure 3.5: A hash collision occurs when different inputs result in the same digest

A good hashing function should be resistant to hash collision; otherwise digital signature forgery becomes possible[4]. Apart from being pre-image resistant, a good hashing function should also be "**second preimage resistant**" i.e. it should not be possible to infer from the current input, a second pre-image that results in the same digest[5].

Apart from SHA265, that was mentioned earlier, other commonly used hashing algorithms include MD5 and SHA-1.

3.6 Merkel Trees

In the preceding chapter, while describing block structure in blockchains, the basic idea behind Merkle trees was presented.

Figure 3.6 serves as a reminder of what Merkle trees look like. The only addition about Merkle trees in this section is their purpose, which is mainly for storage optimization and to speed up verification.

In the case of storage optimization, consider a situation where there is a need to conserve space on storage media for blockchain network nodes. Instead of storing certain kinds of voluminous data on the chain such as videos and images, only the Merkle root hash is stored on the chain, but the files themselves are stored off chain, perhaps on a server somewhere. Recall that what goes on a blockchain is immutable. So the Merkle root hash will be permanently recorded. To know if any of the files have changed, Merkle Root hashing would be performed on them and the result is compared to what is on the blockchain. If it is different then, one file or more must have been altered.

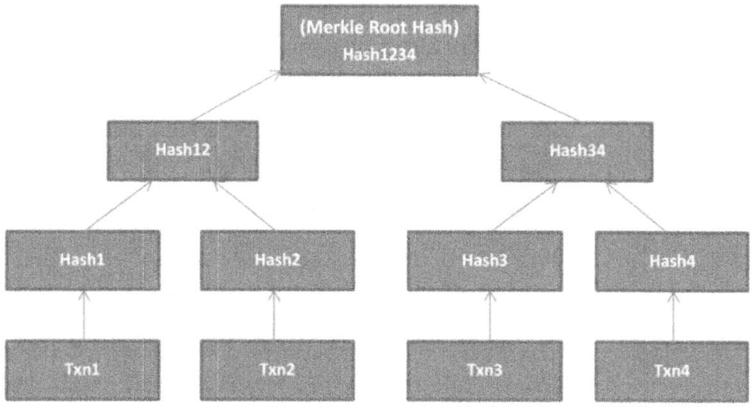

Figure 3.6 Merkle Tree Structure

Regarding verification speed, suppose it is suspected that the integrity of transaction Txn4 has been compromised. It would not be necessary to recalculate hashes for all the other transactions. Only a few data points on the affected side of the Merkle Tree are needed for verification, rather than the whole data set.[12]

3.7 Digital Signatures

Digital signatures serve several purposes. The first one is to give assurance to a receiver of a message that, the source of the message is genuine i.e. the sender is known to the receiver. Secondly, they enable nonrepudiation i.e. the sender cannot later deny sending the message. Lastly, digital signatures assure that the message itself has not been tampered with, on its way to the receiver[6].

To work, a digital signature mechanism must have a signature creation and signature verification components. The signature creation algorithm takes in as input, the sender's private key and the message. The sender's private key is also referred to as the signing key. On the receiving end, the signature verification component takes in as input, the transaction data, the sender's public key and digital signature. Using these three, the signature verification component can determine whether the sender holds the corresponding private key, to the public key the receiver is using. In effect digital signatures provide proof of control of a private key without revealing that private key itself[7].

Figure 3.7 shows how private keys can be used. In the diagram, Bob needs to send a document to Alice. First, Bob creates a hash of the document and then signs (encrypts) the hash with his private key. Then Bob sends both the original document and the signed hash to Alice. Upon receipt, Alice takes the original document and hashes it just like Bob did (using the same algorithm). Let's call the resulting hash X. Then she decrypts the signed hash from Bob using Bob's public key.

Let's call the resulting unencrypted product Y. Finally Alice compares X to Y. If X=Y, then, the document is definitely from Bob (authenticity) and it has not been tampered with (integrity).
Note: These steps occur programmatically using some software.

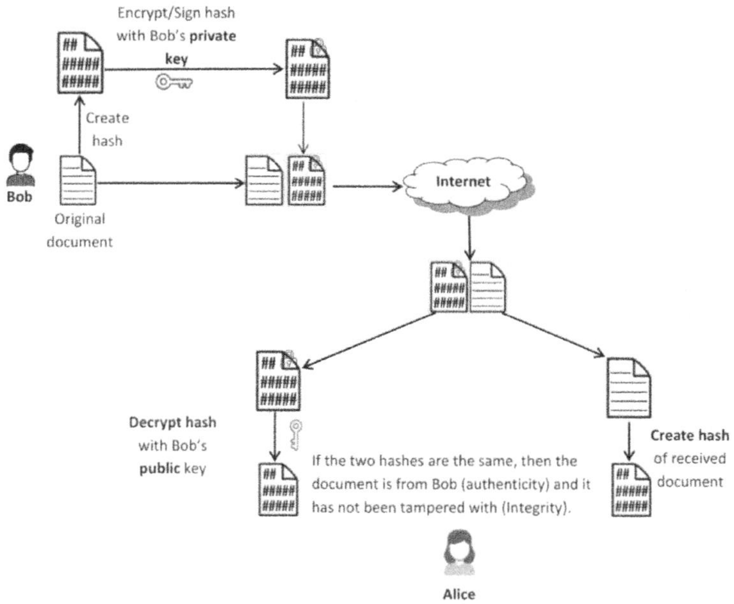

Figure 3.7: Using digital signatures to achieve authenticity, integrity and non-repudiation

In blockchain technology applications, digital signatures are used to verify authorization of sensitive transactions.

3.8 Zero Knowledge Proofs

Cryptography can also be used to confirm that a particular piece of information is true without revealing the information itself. This is called Zero Knowledge Proof (ZKP). For example, instead of providing authentication proof by presenting a signature, in ZKP, a cryptographic proof that the signature is valid is provided[8].

When used in signatures, ZKP reduces the risk of correlation for the signer, thereby shielding the signer from impersonation. This is because it is difficult to link the ZKP to the signer[9]. This is known as **signature blinding**.

There are two types of ZKPs i.e. **challenge response** and **non-interactive**. The former works best when communicating parties are known. Notably challenge response requires an iterative exchange, which could negatively impact performance. Therefore, Non-interactive ZKP is what is most blockchain applications use to prove to the public the validity of something without disclosing information about the transacting parties and/or the transaction[10]. For example in Self Sovereign Identity, blockchain technology can be used to implement a Verifiable Data Registry (VDR) for a revocation list. To enhance privacy, the VDR can use ZKP cryptography that enables verifiers to see the revocation status of a credential in near-real time, but only upon presentation of a proof by a holder. Otherwise the VDR cannot be browsed to see credentials that have been revoked[11].

Conclusion

Cryptography is a very wide topic that involves complex algorithms and mathematics, so this chapter barely scratches the subject's surface.

Chapter two explained how cryptography is used in blockchain block structures to turn transaction information into a digest that serves as a logical "point of connection" for the block that follows. This chapter introduced and explained in simple terms, commonplace terminology used in the blockchain sphere with regards to cryptography. This includes terms like encryption, public and private keys, hashing, digital signatures and cryptographic proofs. How cryptography is used to ensure authenticity, integrity and privacy was also touched on. It should now be clear to the reader that blockchain technology is heavily dependent on cryptography.

The next chapter covers Decentralized Apps, the primary method by which end users access blockchain networks.

Exercise 3

1. Describe a hash tree. Explain what is required to verify that a piece of information exists in a hash tree.

2. In your own words, briefly explain the meaning of authenticity, data integrity and non-repudiation in the context of digital signatures.

3. Familiarize yourself with the following properties of Zero Knowledge Proofs:

   i. Zero-Knowledge

   ii. Completeness

   iii. Soundness

Quiz 3

1 Complete the following statement.
The one who encrypts information is referred to as a ______________________.

a) Stenographer
b) Decipher
c) Cryptanalyst
d) Cryptographer

2 Which of the following statements is **true**?

a) The input to a hashing function is called the pre-image.
b) The output to a hashing function is called the pre-image.
c) Pre-image resistance implies that, using computational brute force, one can determine the resulting digest.
d) Another term for pre-image is digest.

3 Which of the following statement(s) are **false**? (you may choose one or more)

i. In symmetric encryption, the sender and receiver use the same keys for encryption and decryption.
ii. Secure transmission of the decryption key to the sender, is not a problem in symmetric encryption.
iii. Public key encryption is another name for asymmetric encryption.
iv. A message encrypted using a public key must also be decrypted using the same public key to achieve confidentiality.

a) ii and iv
b) i, iii and iv
c) ii only
d) None of the above

4 Which of the following is **not true** regarding hash collisions?

a) A good hashing function should be resistant to hash collision.

b) Hash collisions occur when successful determination of the pre-image can be made from the resulting digest, using computational brute force.
c) Hash collisions occur when several different pre-images result in the same digest.
d) If a hashing function is not resistant to hash collision, then digital signature forgery becomes possible.

5 Which of the following statements **best describes** a hashing function?
a) It is a message digest of a standard size.
b) It is a one way algorithm used in the creation of Merkle Trees.
c) It is an algorithm that takes an input of any size and encrypts it to produce an output of a standard size.
d) It is a one way function.

6 Which of the following statements is **false** concerning digital signatures?
a) Digital signatures enable nonrepudiation.
b) Digital signatures can be used to assure data integrity.
c) A sender signs a message with his public key and the recipient decrypts it with the sender's private.
d) Digital signatures give assurance about the authenticity of a message.

7 Which of the following statements **correctly describes** Zero Knowledge Proof (ZKP)?
a) It is a way of proving that a statement is valid, and both the statement and proof is presented.
b) It is part of public key cryptography since there no knowledge of the private key.
c) It is part of public key cryptography since there no knowledge of the public key.
d) It is a way of proving that a statement is valid, but without revealing anything besides the validity of the statement.

8 In order to verify that some specific information is encrypted inside a hash tree, what would be necessary? (you may choose one or more)

i. The hashes found along the root path.
ii. The Merkle root hash.
iii. Digital signature
iv. The leaf hash

a) iii only
b) ii only
c) i, ii and iv
d) ii and iv

9 Fill in the blanks.
In the past, the two common methods used to handle encryption were ____________ and ______________.

a) transposition, decryption
b) substitution, transposition
c) substitution, decryption
d) transposition, teleportation

10 Which of the following statements describes "second pre-image resistance"?

a) When a hashing algorithm can infer from the current input, a second pre-image that results in the same digest.
b) When a hashing algorithm cannot infer from the current input, a second pre-image that results in the same digest.
c) When a hashing algorithm cannot infer from the current output, a second pre-image that results in the same digest.
d) When a hashing algorithm can infer from the current input, a second pre-image that results in the same hash value.

References

1 Kumar, N., Gayathri, N., Rahman, Md. A., & Balamurugan, B. (Eds.). (2020). *Blockchain, Big Data and Machine Learning* (p. 2). CRC Press.

2 Lemieux, V. L., & Feng, C. (2021). *Building Decentralized Trust* (p. 68). Springer Nature.

3 Hellwig, D., Karlic, G., & Huchzermeier, A. (2020). *Build Your Own Blockchain* (pp. 125, 127-129). Springer International Publishing.

4 Antonopoulos, A. M., & Wood, G. (2018). *Mastering Ethereum* (pp. 164, 165). O'Reilly Media.

5 Hellwig, D., Karlic, G., & Huchzermeier, A. (2020). *Build Your Own Blockchain* (p. 133). Springer International Publishing.

6 M. C., & Lupien, S. C. (2022). *Blockchain Fundamentals for Web 3.0* (pp. 104-105). University of Arkansas Press.

7 Antonopoulos, A. M., & Wood, G. (2018). *Mastering Ethereum* (pp. 235, 233). O'Reilly Media.

8 Lacity, M. C., & Lupien, S. C. (2022). *Blockchain Fundamentals for Web 3.0* (p. 379). University of Arkansas Press.

9 Preukschat, A., & Reed, D. (2021). *SELF-SOVEREIGN IDENTITY : decentralized digital identity and verifiable credentials.* (pp. 122, 123). O'reilly Media.

10 Lacity, M. C., & Lupien, S. C. (2022). *Blockchain Fundamentals for Web 3.0* (pp. 379-381). University of Arkansas Press.

11 Preukschat, A., & Reed, D. (2021). *SELF-SOVEREIGN IDENTITY : decentralized digital identity and verifiable credentials.* (p. 201). O'reilly Media.

12 Zundel, B. and Zouarhi, S. (2021). Basic cryptography techniques for SSI. In: *SELF-SOVEREIGN IDENTITY : decentralized digital identity and verifiable credentials.* S.L.: O'reilly Media, pp.117–119.

13 Daphne, T. (2022). *Zero-knowledge proofs explained in 3 examples.* [online] www.circularise.com. Available at:

https://www.circularise.com/blogs/zero-knowledge-proofs-explained-in-3-examples [Accessed 11 Apr. 2025].

4. Decentralized Applications

"As far as the customer is concerned, the interface is the product"
- Jef Raskin

4.1 Introduction

From the previous chapters in this book, you know that a Blockchain is a distributed ledger technology and have seen that transactions are stored in a decentralized manner. What has not been covered is how to access this data that is spread out across many devices. This is the subject of discussion in this chapter.

Decentralized applications are also referred to as decentralized apps. They are also abbreviated as Dapps, or DApps, or dApps. To understand them, let us first appreciate what a centralized application system is.

4.2 Centralized Applications

As depicted in figure 4.1, in a centralized system, the clients run an application that is hosted at one location.

Ideally, a centralized system belongs to a single entity such as a government agency or a business or even an individual. The application server could be located either on the entity's own premises or with a cloud services provider [1].

For storage and retrieval of data, a centralized application may use either local storage on the same computer or other remote facilities. Whatever the case, the key issue here is that, there is just one application interface which clients use to access services as intended by the service provider i.e. application system owner. Whereas this portends a single point of failure

(SPoF), there are ways to mitigate such problems. However, such solutions are beyond the scope of this book.

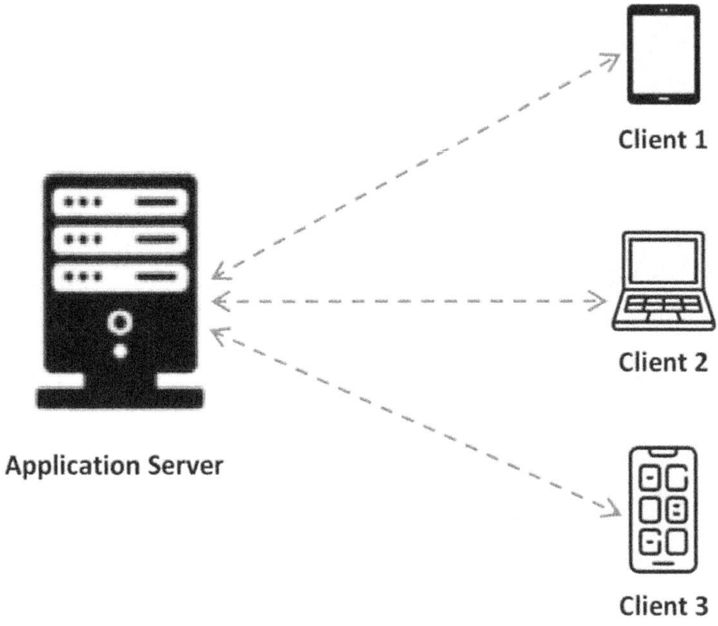

Figure 4.1: Centralized Application system

Prior to discussing decentralized systems, it is important that we also look briefly at distributed systems, which can easily be confused with the former, because they both run on more than one server/computer.

4.3 Distributed Applications

A distributed system presents itself to clients like a single system, however in reality there are a group of networked computers working together to provide the required service as depicted in figure 4.2.

Just like in a centralized system, the owner of a distributed system servers is likely to be a single entity.

Each server in the distributed system may have a specialized role that contributes to the success of the unified service provided to a client. Alternatively, they could be performing the same roles but balancing work load among themselves, thereby improving on efficiency.

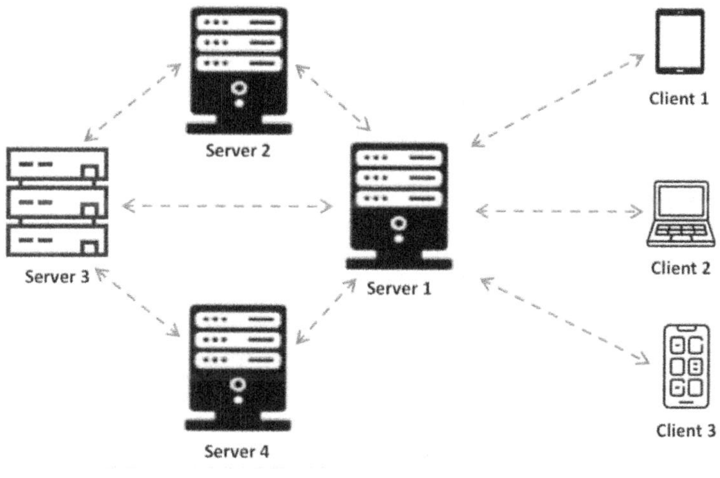

Figure 4.2: Distributed Application system

In situations where the servers in a distributed system are geographically dispersed, it is expected that a server's work load will mostly consist of clients in close proximity to it.

The drawbacks of distributed systems are that they are more difficult to setup, secure and administer. Also, even though typical distributed systems are not usually within a single location, they are likely to be under one central authority just like centralized systems. The import of this is that the clients must trust the authorities offering services through these architectures. Unfortunately, centralized authorities have proved themselves to be unworthy of trust[2].

This issue of trust is one of the problems that blockchain technology was intended to solve, and that's why it is referred to as a "trustless" system. Trustless here implies that, participants need not know each other for the system to work fairly, and in an expected manner. In other words, blockchain technologies "allow trust even if the counterparty is not known"[2].

4.4 Decentralized Applications

Figure 4.3 depicts a blockchain network. Recall that all nodes participating in the network are peers i.e. there is no server.

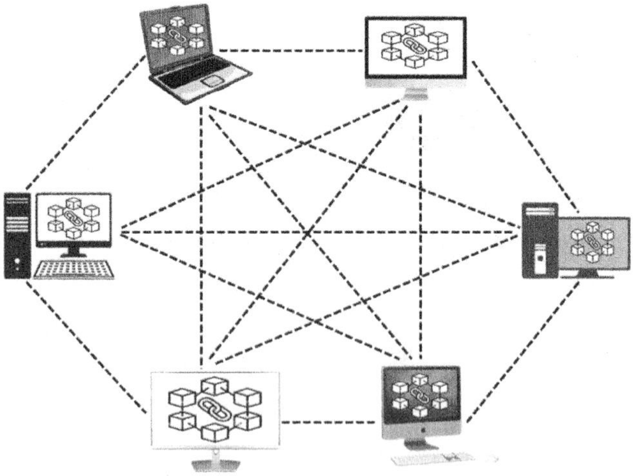

Figure 4.3: Blockchain Network

In the same manner that blocks are replicated on every participating node, DApps are also replicated on each node of a blockchain network. And an "on chain" feature exists that allows any individual to scrutinize the DApp code, in order to ascertain its functionality. The rationale for this is that the more copies of DApps, running the exact same code, on different nodes under the control of different authorities, the more trustworthy the network is[5]. DApps also take advantage of the other benefits of blockchain such as immutability, security and resilience.

The first functional or successful blockchain network i.e. Bitcoin network, was intended primarily for transferring bitcoin (cryptocurrency) from one account to another. It had a limited use case and was difficult to customize. Later, a general purpose programmable blockchain called Ethereum was built. General purpose here means a network that supports various types, and numerous applications beyond simple transfer of value, like on the Bitcoin network.

For clarity, if one hears of the Bitcoin network, their imagination is likely to be limited to bitcoin transactions. However, in the case of Ethereum network, even though it has a native cryptocurrency called Ether, which generally speaking functions like bitcoin (interacted with using a "financial" DApp), it also runs many other applications created by independent developers, who are not part of the core development team of the Ethereum network[3]. These applications' use cases range from supply chain management to gaming, finance, identity management, advertising etc[4]. So, general purpose blockchain networks like Ethereum serve as platforms for running decentralized applications. Other similar networks include Polkadot and Solana.

4.5 Anatomy of a DApp

In their book, "*Mastering Ethereum*", Antonopoulos and Wood aptly describe a DApp as "a web application that is built on top of open, decentralized, peer-to-peer infrastructure services." More specifically, it is one or more smart contracts, accessible via various means, though a web user interface is more common[6].

Smart contracts are covered in more detail in the next chapter. For now, just think of smart contracts as a type of program i.e. lines of code to accomplish some objective e.g. business logic.

Figure 4.4 illustrates how a client (end user) would interact with a DApp. Just in case you are wondering, the backend of a DApp is typically written using languages like Solidity, Vyper, Rust or Golang. The language selected will definitely depend on the Blockchain network you intend to run your DApp on.

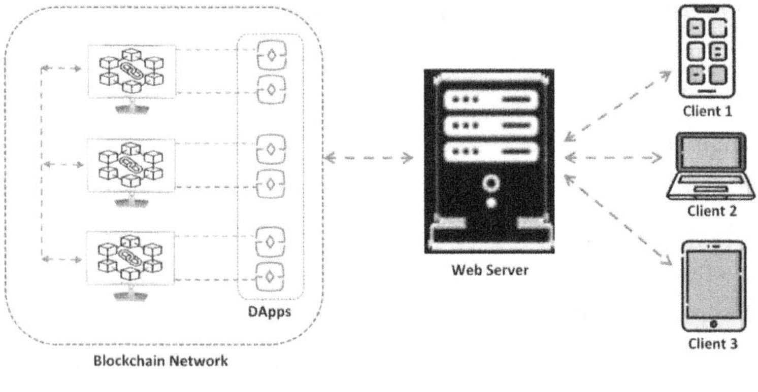

Figure 4.4: Client interaction with a Decentralized Application[7]

The webserver would interact remotely with the DApps using Web3.js JavaScript library. The tools used for the front end are the normal ones for developing a web based user interface. These include Python, JavaScript, CSS and of course HTML[8].

Finally the end user just needs a browser to interact with the DApp(s) indirectly.

I have mentioned the examples of languages used to code the backend, but not the source code editors i.e. the tools into which you write the actual programming logic for the DApps before compiling them. These too, are also available in a large variety. For example, consider Solidity, which is used to code DApps for the Etherium Blockchain network. Not only can we use Remix, an online editor, but there are already a number of generic Integrated Development Environments (IDEs) that support the solidity plugin. These include Atom, Emacs, Visual Studio Code, Sublime and Vi. There are also a number of frameworks which can be used to develop smart contracts for the Ethereum platform, such as Truffle, Embark and others [9].

Note:

An **IDE** just makes it easier for a programmer to write code in the correct manner. For example, it may have basic features like autocomplete for keywords, different colors for different program elements and will usually underline syntax mistakes in the program. Such features reduce the amount of time spent writing and debugging code.

Plugins are used to extend the capabilities of an IDE, so that it can support an additional language (framework) e.g. to work with C++, you install a C++ plugin, if it is supported, but not installed by default.

A **framework** is a software abstraction that increases the efficiency of a programmer by allowing him to specify requirements at a higher level and the details are then generated by the framework. Frameworks also allow a programmer to concentrate on the unique aspects of the project, while standard components are generated automatically.

4.6 DApp Use Cases

Among the first and also most obvious examples of DApps are cryptocurrency wallets. These are user interface tools that are used to interact with a blockchain network when transferring cryptocurrency from peer to peer[9]. As a natural progression, beyond crypto wallets, majority of the DApps that came after, were somehow related to Decentralized Finance (DeFi) i.e. financial transactions on blockchains revolving around activities like lending, banking and investing.

However, since the entry of general purpose blockchains like Ethereum, there has been a huge increase in the number of DApps whose primary purpose is to facilitate other business objectives besides finance. For example, the Supply Chain industry noticed that blockchain technology is a potent tool for provenance tracking. Consider organic beef sold at a shop. Using blockchain technology, it can be tracked back to the locations it came through i.e. distribution center, facility where it was processed, right to the farm where the cow or bull was raised. The fact that consumers can verify origins, gives some of them confidence that what they are paying for, is what has been advertised. Such consumers might prefer brands that facilitate provenance over those that do not, and might even be willing to pay a little extra money for their goods.

When Bitcoin was first rolled out, there was talk about that period being a defining new stage for the internet and the phrase "internet of money" was being bandied about. But as other new use cases for blockchain technology became apparent, some groups came up with the phrase "internet of identities", because they envisioned DApps that can be used to store and present personal information on a need to know basis. The presented information can be verified by intended recipients, cryptographically, using blockchain as a Verifiable

Data Registry under the control of a trusted authority. This is the subject of discussion in chapter 8 of this book, under the title "Self-Sovereign Identity".

In chapter 7, Non-Fungible Tokens and how they can be used to facilitate fractional ownership is covered. Obviously there are DApps that are used to manage these tokens as well. Suffice it to say that currently available DApps are not just too many to cover in a book, leave alone a chapter, but new ones are being created regularly, and some older ones are being discarded as better ones come into the market. You can explore examples of DApps on the "dapp list" found @ https://thedapplist.com/.

Some of the DApps being released, that run on top of general purpose blockchains have their own native coin or crypto token. For example recall that Ethereum's native crypto token is Ether (ETH). Yet other applications that are themselves about crypto tokens run on the same blockchain. This includes cryptocurrencies like Tether, USDC, BNB etc.

However, on the Ethereum network, in order to forestall Denial of Service attacks (DoS), every transaction executed on it, has to be paid for in Ether. This means that it would cost an attacker real money in order to be destructive.

Note: In a DoS, a malicious attacker overwhelms a server by engaging it in a continuous and relentless manner, until it can no longer provide service to genuine clients.

The Ether that is charged for transactions is also used to maintain services on the network such as compensating transaction validators. The amount charged depends on the current network traffic as well as the nature of the transaction[11].

4.7 Oracles

Consider a simple DApp that manages bets between two parties. Specifically, it holds money (crypto) in escrow before the bet, and then immediately and automatically pays out the money to the winner of the bet, as soon as the event that determines the outcome occurs.

Suppose Tom says it will rain at 6pm and Mary says that it will not. Both Tom and Mary can pay out crypto equivalent to 10 dollars to the DApp which then holds the total money on their behalf. If it rains at 6pm, it pays Tom 20$ in the relevant crypto. Otherwise, the DApp sends 20$ to Mary. It will be easy for the DApp to know that it is 6pm from the computer system clock, but how will it know whether it rained at 6pm or not? This information is not inside the blockchain.

DApps by design, only work with resources within the network due to trust and technical issues. In order for a DApp to receive external information such as weather data, a program known as an Oracle is required.

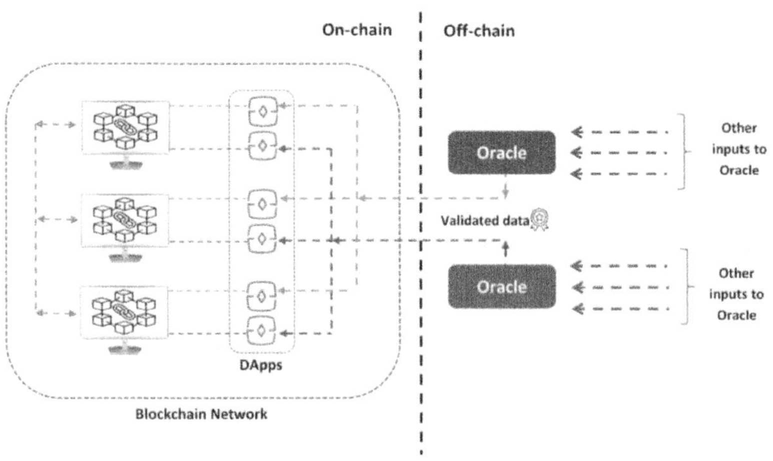

Figure 4.5: Oracle interaction with Decentralized Applications[13]

Figure 4.5 depicts the interaction of two oracles with two decentralized applications. An Oracle is like a bridge between the world outside a blockchain and the blockchain itself. An Oracle must be fed by trust worthy data suppliers, and ideally, whenever it is passing data to a blockchain, the data should be accompanied by some proof of authenticity and integrity[12].

So in the Tom and Mary example, slightly past 6pm, an oracle will pass weather data to the DApp in the blockchain, which will then decide who to send the money to.

Conclusion

DApps are in a sense, applications built for individuals and businesses to facilitate access to blockchain networks in order to interact with them and thus enjoy the benefits that the blockchain technologies inherently offer. This includes resilience, transparency and censorship resistance.

The next chapter is about Smart Contracts, which are the building blocks for decentralized applications. If DApps are books, then Smart Contracts are pages.

Exercise 4

1. Research on, and then briefly describe how DApps can be used for regulatory auditing work.

2. Using Augur as an example, research on, and then briefly describe how Decentralized prediction markets work.

3. List examples of DApps for Crowdfunding and the blockchain network they operate on e.g. WeiFund on Ethereum.

i. ____

ii. ____

iii. ____

iv. ____

v. ____

Quiz 4

1 Which of the following statements is **true**?

a) With decentralized applications the clients run an application that is hosted on one server.

b) Centralized and distributed systems are typically owned by several entities.

c) With distributed applications the clients run an application that is hosted on one server.

d) Centralized and distributed systems are typically owned by one entity.

2 Fill in the blanks.

A ______________________ application system presents itself to clients like a single system, even though it could be spread across two or more networked computers, working together to provide a required service.

a) Blockchain

b) Decentralized

c) Distributed

d) Centralized

3 Which of the following statements describes decentralized application systems?

a) Decentralized applications are replicated on the best servers of a blockchain network.

b) Decentralized applications are installed on a single server to enhance trust in the network.

c) Decentralized applications are replicated on each node of a blockchain network.

d) Decentralized applications on a blockchain are black boxes since it is nearly impossible to inspect their source code.

4 Which of the following statements are **false**? (you may choose one or more)

i. In comparison to centralized application systems, distributed applications are easier to secure.

ii. Both centralized and distributed application systems are usually under the control of a single entity.
iii. Both centralized and distributed application systems require that the clients trust the service providers.
iv. Distributed application systems are highly likely to be under the control of several entities.

a) i and iv
b) i and ii
c) ii, iii and iv
d) ii and iii

5 Fill in the blanks.
An ___________________ feature exists that allows any individual to scrutinize a DApp's code in order to ascertain its functionality.

a) Oracle
b) on chain
c) off chain
d) decentralized

6 Which of the following statements is **false**?

a) DApps take advantage of the inherent benefits of blockchain networks such as immutability, security and resilience.
b) Ethereum network was intended primarily for transferring ether (cryptocurrency) from one account to another.
c) Bitcoin network was intended primarily for transferring bitcoin (cryptocurrency) from one account to another.
d) The more copies of DApps running the exact same code on different nodes under the control of different entities, the more trustworthy the network is.

7 Which of the following **least** describes a decentralized application?

a) A DApp is a cryptocurrency wallet.
b) A DApp is any smart contract with a web frontend[15].

c) A DApp is a web application that is built on top of open, decentralized, peer-to-peer infrastructure services[6].

d) A DApp is based on business logic encapsulated into smart contracts that are executed against a distributed database called blockchain[14].

8 Which of the following statements is **true**?

a) The backend of a DApp is typically coded using languages like Solidity, HTML, Rust or JavaScript.

b) The frontend of a DApp is typically coded using languages like Solidity, HTML, or JavaScript.

c) The backend of a DApp is typically coded using languages like JavaScript, CSS and HTML.

d) The backend of a DApp is typically coded using languages like Solidity, Vyper, Rust or Golang.

9 Complete the following statement.

A webserver hosting the frontend of a DApp can interact remotely with the DApp using the ____________________.

a) Web.js HTML library

b) Solidity library

c) Web3.js JavaScript library

d) Vyper library

10 Which of the following statements are **true**? (you may choose one or more)

i. By design, DApps cannot work with resources within the blockchain network due to technical and trust issues.

ii. By design, DApps only work with resources within the blockchain network due to technical and trust issues.

iii. A program known as Golang is required so that a DApp can receive information external to its native blockchain network.

iv. A program known as an Oracle is required so that a DApp can receive information external to its native blockchain network.

a) ii and iv
b) ii only
c) i and iii
d) None of the above

References

1 Infante, R. (2019). *Building Ethereum Dapps: Decentralized Applications on the Ethereum Blockchain.* Manning Incorporated, p. 41.

2 Lemieux, V.L. and Feng, C. eds., (2021). *Building Decentralized Trust.* Springer Nature, pp. 1, 83.

3 Burniske, C. and Tatar, J. (2018). *Cryptoassets : The Innovative Investor's Guide to Bitcoin and Beyond /.* New York, N.Y.: Mcgraw-Hill Education, p.138.

4 Cryptopedia Staff (2025). *What Is Ethereum Blockchain; and its Key Use Cases?* [online] Gemini. Available at: https://www.gemini.com/cryptopedia/ethereum-smart-contracts-tokens-use-cases [Accessed 2 Jun. 2025].

5 Infante, R. (2019). *Building Ethereum Dapps: Decentralized Applications on the Ethereum Blockchain.* Manning Incorporated, pp. 58-59.

6 Antonopoulos, A.M. and Wood Ph.D, G. (2018). *Mastering Ethereum.* O'Reilly Media, p. 60.

7 Stohniiev, H. (2024). *How to Build a Dapp on Ethereum Blockchain?* [online] IdeaSoft. Available at: https://ideasoft.io/blog/how-to-develop-dapp-on-ethereum/ [Accessed 3 Jun. 2025].

8 Weston, G. (2025). *Top Languages For Dapp Developers in 2025.* [online] 101 Blockchains. Available at: https://101blockchains.com/top-languages-for-dapp-developers/ [Accessed 3 Jun. 2025].

9 Infante, R. (2019). *Building Ethereum Dapps: Decentralized Applications on the Ethereum Blockchain.* Manning Incorporated, pp. 417, 120.

10 thedapplist.com. (n.d.). *The Dapp List | Explore community-curated Web3 projects.* [online] Available at: https://thedapplist.com/ [Accessed 6 Jun. 2025].

11 Burniske, C. and Tatar, J. (2018). *Cryptoassets : The Innovative*

Investor's Guide to Bitcoin and Beyond /. New York, N.Y.: Mcgraw-Hill Education, p.140.

12 Infante, R. (2019). *Building Ethereum Dapps: Decentralized Applications on the Ethereum Blockchain.* Manning Incorporated, pp. 410-411.

13 CSIRO (2023). *Oracle - Blockchain Patterns.* [online] Blockchain Patterns. Available at: https://research.csiro.au/blockchainpatterns/general-patterns/interacting-with-the-external-world/oracle/ [Accessed 6 Jun. 2025].

14 Infante, R. (2019). *Building Ethereum Dapps: Decentralized Applications on the Ethereum Blockchain.* Manning Incorporated, p. 87.

15 Antonopoulos, A.M. and Wood Ph.D, G. (2018). *Mastering Ethereum.* O'Reilly Media, pp. 496, 497.

5. Smart Contracts

"Blockchain is the tech. Bitcoin is merely the first mainstream manifestation of its potential."
—Marc Kenigsberg

5.1 Introduction

As mentioned in the previous chapter, sometime after the release of Bitcoin blockchain, it was noticed that the underlying technology could lend itself to other uses besides the simple transfer of value, like in the case of bitcoin. One of these areas is in contracting.

In its simplest form, a contract is an agreement between one or more parties. Typically, one or all the parties to a contract have one or more obligations (actions) which are to be carried out under certain circumstances (conditions).

When the word contract is used, people are likely to think of legal documents involving lawyers. However, it must be noted that in our daily lives, we engage in many agreements with other parties which are informal in the sense that an actual contract document might either, not exist, or, they might exist, but in a form that is not straight forward e.g. when you book and pay for a birthday cake to be delivered on a certain date. You have a contract with your baker. Your obligation is to pay, if you placed an order, and the baker's obligation is to bake a cake according to an agreed specification. In this case, the evidence/contract documents are the purchase orders, payment receipts, delivery notes, etc.

The point here is that there are many contracts that individuals and businesses engage in, that do not typically require lawyers, unless and until a dispute arises, and the only recourse is in a courtroom. Some of these contracts could be inter departmental within the same business organization e.g. production department agrees with transport department that, once new products reach a certain threshold, they should be moved to some distant warehouse. Some of these contracts are therefore just business processes, or business rules that could be computerized.

Nevertheless for the purposes of our discussion, let's take note of the fact that a contract has two important components. The first one is condition or state e.g. "New products have reached 1,000 units". The second component is action (obligation) e.g. "Transport them to the warehouse". So the general structure of the simplest contract can be summarized as "if condition, then action".

The condition in a contract may be influenced by one of the contracting parties e.g. "if customer pays, shopkeeper releases goods". Here, the customer and shopkeeper are the contracting parties. It is the customer who affects the state of payment and the shopkeeper has the obligation to release the concerned goods, if the state of payment changes from "Not paid" to "paid". In other scenarios, the condition could be influenced by an independent external entity such as the weather, or game outcome.

It is normal to expect that somewhere along the line, contract agreements might be breached. In his work "Leviathan", Thomas Hobbes attributes contract disputes to human nature by stating that,

> "For he that performed first has no assurance the other will perform after, because the bonds of words are too weak to bridle men's ambition, avarice, anger, and other passions, without the fear of some coercive power"[1].

However, sometimes contract disputes stem from the difficulty in determining whether condition(s) that trigger obligations were met. In addition or alternatively, the difficulty could be about measuring the adequacy of the obligation carried out[2]. Within an organization, contract breaches are likely to be interpreted as some sort of incompetence and could lead to dismissal. In a business environment, contracts are usually written down and signed as evidence of agreement, so that in case one party fails to honor their end of the agreement and an amicable solution cannot be arrived at, then courts can be used to try and resolve the issue, sometimes by enforcing compliance.

Now, as more personal and businesses transactions move to the digital world, one of the problems to contend with, is the ease with which information can easily be altered, sometimes without being detected until much later when some form of damage has already taken place. In our context, such alterations could be made with the intention of justifying or engineering a contract breach. This is where blockchain technology comes in, armed with its properties of immutability and provenance[3]. Whereas this would help in the preservation of the integrity of the "contract rules", what about "contract party obligations" ?

Well, if the rules can be codified and obligations can be fulfilled automatically by means of digital transactions, and there is a way of representing transactions for different contracting parties, then you have what is known as a smart contract.

5.2 Smart Contract Definition

It might surprise the reader that the term "smart contract" predates the Bitcoin blockchain by over a decade. In 1994, Nick

Szabo, known to be the originator of the term "smart contract", wrote a paper where he described it as "a computerized transaction protocol that executes the terms of a contract"[4].

So a smart contract is not a legally binding contract that has to be presided over by a lawyer. Rather it is a computer program implementation of the rules and obligations specified in a contract[5].

As a piece of software code, a smart contract will therefore store the conditions that determine predefined actions and the actions themselves. During execution, smart contracts verify the conditions and then carry out the relevant predefined action(s) for the prevailing condition[6].

It should be noted that because smart contracts are stored on a blockchain, they are duplicated on all the nodes on the blockchain. This redundancy makes smart contract resilient because if some nodes on the network become unavailable, the program will still be accessible on others. Furthermore, the chaining of blocks makes smart contracts tamper evident.

It should also be noted that because the "actions" of a smart contract are actually in the form of transactions that change the state of the blockchain, they have to be verified independently by validating nodes on the blockchain network like any other transaction before being accepted into a block. Then using a consensus mechanism, a block containing a "smart contract generated" transaction may be accepted onto the chain[7].

In section 4.7 of the last chapter, an example of a smart contract was given, but it was referred to it as a DApp. In the example, Tom agrees to pay Mary 10 dollars if it rains today at 6pm. Mary also agrees to pay Tom 10 dollars if it DOES NOT rain today at 6pm. It is a simple bet, an agreement – a contract, which can go wrong. Either party could refuse to pay the other, if the weather condition at 6pm implies that they will become short of 10 dollars. Tom and Mary could solidify this agreement and have a written and signed contract. This could help depending on the nature of the two. What happens if either party still refuses to pay out ? What would it cost to claim one's dues in terms of time and money (legal help, transport, communication costs)? Is it worth it?

Suppose it did not rain at 6 pm, a written and signed contract exists and Mary knows that Tom is too busy, or too broke, or too proud to pursue the matter, or all of the aforementioned. Mary won't pay Tom his dues and the matter ends there.

This kind of problem has existed with mankind and the common solution for handling it is to introduce a "neutral" third party in such contract arrangements. In our example, both Tom and Mary can deposit into an escrow account, 10$ together with a copy of the contract with John, the "neutral" third party. So, if it rains at 6pm, John is supposed to pay Mary 20$. On the other hand, if it does not rain, John is supposed to pay Tom 20$.

On the surface, the problem seems sorted, but it isn't. Not only will John refuse to do this for free, but we have transferred our "human integrity" concerns from Tom and Mary to John. So even if Tom and Mary each deposit 11$ with John, to take care of his fee, John could still spend part or all of the 20$ before 6pm and then ask the beneficiary to wait for some unspecified period before receiving his/her dues. Another concern is, what if Mary and John have some relationship (even indirectly), that Tom is unaware of, and it does not rain at 6pm and then John decides to give back to both parties 10$ each, instead of paying Tom 20$? If Tom has the wherewithal to go to court, his case will be a bit more complex. One could argue that professional institutions don't act like John, but that would be so naïve, because institutions depend on the character of its employees and over time, good employees could easily be replaced by others of questionable value systems. Moreover, whereas I am using examples of 20$ debts, in business, we would be talking about 5 or more zeros at the end i.e. 2 to 20 million dollars or even more.

Now consider a smart contract that just checks programmatically that Tom and Mary have each deposited 10$ into its account and then it waits for 6pm and finally automatically pays either Tom or Mary, depending on received weather data. Neither Tom nor Mary can request their money back once they have deposited it. The smart contract has no loans to pay, no medical emergencies, and has no girlfriend or nagging wife to impress. One cannot blackmail it, bribe it, or beg it for a favor. If designed properly, it will NOT misappropriate funds !!!

Smart contracts do not require a middleman because they can autonomously execute codified agreements on a blockchain[8]. Moreover, this autonomous execution makes legal enforcement unnecessary. In our example, if it does not rain at 6pm, the contract just sends to Tom, Mary's money. Mary does not have to be asked for permission or even be coerced to pay. By placing her money in escrow with the smart contract, Mary assented to the possibility that it would be paid to Tom, if he won the bet. So, smart contracts ensure that once a promise is made, that promise will be fulfilled expeditiously[9].

5.3 Legal vs Smart Contracts

A legally enforceable contract serves as a security document that only comes into play if there are grievances **ex post** (after the contract reference period). Whereas the contract document is likely to create motivations for compliance, the key thing to note here is that, its existence does not preclude the possibility of contract beaches. So, when one or more of the contract parties fail to meet their obligations, courts act as remedial institutions i.e. try to enforce compliance.

Contrast this with smart contracts, which by design have no possibility of contract breaches and therefore eliminate the necessity for remediation especially in many business related scenarios.

Fundamentally, they both serve the same underlying function, which is to ensure that contract obligations are carried out. In legalese, contract law does this via "**ex post adjudication**", while smart contracts do this via "**ex ante enforcement**".

But ex post adjudication's objective is different. It is to identify grievances and then resolve them. This can be costly in terms of time and money. Ex ante enforcement's objective on the other hand is to act as an agent of the contracting parties and to actually carry out their obligations.

Let's revisit the weather betting example involving Tom and Mary. It is so simple that it gives room for contentions to arise even if a smart contract is employed to enforce it. For example, suppose after the bet, Tom travelled to a location 3 hours away from Mary. Let's further suppose that it rains where Mary is but does not rain where Tom is. Finally, let's say that the smart contract sends money to Tom using data that claims that it did not rain near Mary. Clearly, Mary will not be amused. If it were not for the amounts involved, I suspect that Mary would lawyer up. The smart contract will then be subject to ex post litigation in a traditional court. This example serves to tell us that smart contracts are still legally enforceable contracts because as agents of parties, under certain circumstances, they might shift value, rights and obligations in a manner that may not be satisfactory to all relevant parties[9].

Considering the scenario in the preceding paragraph, a trusted third party might decide to render the agreement null and void, and return money to both Tom and Mary, even if such provisions were not made for in advance. Contract law courts also, might be able to see, *ex post,* when some obligations are either unfair or unenforceable. A smart contract is not that smart or creative – it rigidly does only what it is programmed to do[10].

Suffice it to say that whereas smart contracts can minimize the need for contract litigation in some scenarios, they cannot be replacements for contract law and lawyers.

5.4 Types of Smart Contracts

Smart contracts are currently categorized based on the source of the information that they work with.

If after deployment the smart contract never requires information from outside its host blockchain for execution, then it is called a **deterministic smart contract**.

Conversely, a **non-deterministic smart contract** is one that requires information from outside its host blockchain to operate[5]. This information is delivered via oracles, a mechanism for entering operational data into a blockchain[6]. The data from oracles is meant to improve on the quality of decision making by the smart contract[10].

Note: Oracles were covered in the preceding chapter.

5.5 Technical Overview of Smart Contracts

If you are already familiar with object-oriented programming (OOP) concepts and languages like C++ or Java, then the learning curve for writing smart contracts using Solidity, would be pleasantly shallow for you.

Since a smart contract is software code, it consists of lines of instructions that verify contract conditions, as well those that execute specified actions. These instructions are organized in units similar to classes in OOP languages. Classes in OOP contain one or more methods which are just logical groupings of instructions to achieve specific objectives. With smart contracts, methods are called functions. Otherwise, concepts like encapsulation, inheritance, polymorphism, method overriding and abstraction, generally apply to smart contracts as well, albeit with slight differences.

Like in other OOP languages, modifiers can be used in smart contract functions to control how they work. Similarly modifiers can also be used on variables and functions to control visibility scopes. In Solidity there are four visibility scope modifiers i.e. private, public, internal and external. (In case you are wondering, variables are for storing the data necessary for implementing the logic of the smart contract)[11].

Anyway, once a smart contract has been written using a high level language such as Solidity, it has to be compiled before deployment. The compiler's output will be in the form of Ethereum Virtual Machine bytecode (EVM bytecode). Secondly, it has to be registered on the blockchain network. To do this, the developer must signify that he wants to register a contract's EVM bytecode on the Ethereum blockchain, by creating a special transaction whose destination must be specified as the **zero address**. The zero address looks like "0x0000000000000000000000000000000000000000". This registration of EVM bytecode is known as the **contract deployment transaction.**

The contract deployment transaction first executes on the local Ethereum node, and then propagates peer to peer, all over the network. As each mining node receives the deployment transaction, it is processed. As with other transactions, a smart contract's EVM bytecode will only be stored on the blockchain, when a new block containing it is accepted as the next block, by a consensus mechanism.

On the Ethereum blockchain, deployed contracts have Ethereum addresses, just like cryptocurrency wallets. To run the smart contract on the EVM, a transaction should be sent to the contract address. This transaction can contain ether, or data, or both. If it contains data, in addition to the data, a function within the contract should be specified to process it. Obviously, the data will be presented as parameters passed to the function. Otherwise, if it is just ether, then a function designed to update the smart contract's balance will handle it[12, 13].

For those who are not familiar with programming, do not be dismayed if you find this section unsettling. Normally, a programmer would build a user friendly interface (web interface), with labels and appropriate input widgets for interacting with the smart contract. This eliminates the need for most users to know the inner workings of a smart contract. However, since blockchain technology is also about transparency, any individual who is more technically inclined should be able to scrutinize the source code of a smart contract deployed on a blockchain. (You might want to have another look at section 4.5 of the preceding chapter – Anatomy of a DApp).

5.6 Purpose of Smart Contracts

Most readers will be familiar with standard contract forms (SCFs). These are a set of terms and conditions that some business issue to their customers, mostly on photo copied paper. Every customer is presented with the exact same terms and conditions in order to save time and money for the business. Typically, the terms and conditions on such contracts are determined by one party (the business) and the other party (the customer), either accepts the agreement by signing on the paper or rejects the agreement by walking away.

In a sense, smart contracts are like SCFs because they are intended for scenarios that target a large number of entities. Therefore, smart contracts can be used by both businesses and government to streamline their operations[14].

Smart contracts can also be owned by individuals or groups of people or by absolutely no one. The rules or contract terms will depend on the intended usage. Obviously, the complexity will vary. If you consider that technically, a smart contract can be made to call other smart contracts, then a single execution of a specific contract can lead to a chain reaction on a blockchain network. Apart from transferring cryptocurrencies, smart contracts can also be used to represent and manage transfer of ownership, or fractional ownership of real world physical assets such as real estate. Other uses include voting and management of Identity Systems[15, 16].

5.7 Decentralized Autonomous Organization

As discussed earlier, a smart contract can be used to carry out actions or obligations as an agent of an entity. We are also aware that they were originally used for transferring cryptocurrency. So if smart contracts can also be used for voting, incrementally, we should be able to see the possibility of smart contracts being designed to carry out the role of a legal corporate organization without physical structures like an office or personnel. This is what we call a Decentralized Autonomous Organization (DAO).

A DAO is completely composed of software code. Its operations are governed by rules written in the software code and its address is the address assigned to it on the blockchain hosting it[17]. The allure to DAOs is that, unlike human run organizations, it is more trustworthy because it is easier to predict and to audit. DAOs actions are consistent, while human employee actions are dependent on character or state of mind and many other subjective issues[18].

It must be noted that DAO smart contracts are written by human beings, and if not done properly could lead to losses for the owners of the organization.

5.8 Advantages of Smart Contracts

We can summarize Smart contracts advantages with the following statements.

1) Smart contracts preempt the possibility of disappointment arising from failure by one or more parties in fulfilling their obligation.
2) Because they are stored on a blockchain, smart contracts, just like transactions on blockchains, are immutable.
3) Compared to non-digital contracts, smart contracts are more efficient in terms of speed and objectivity. Add scalability, and cost savings also becomes a selling point.
4) Smart contracts lower the risk of collaboration because their functionality is predictable, transparent and independently verifiable by scrutinizing the source code.

5) Smart contracts are trustless systems where the contracting parties need not know each other for a successful outcome. There is no requirement for a trusted third party to monitor or enforce contract execution either.

5.9 Disadvantages of Smart Contracts

The term smart contract is actually a misnomer because smart contracts only execute what is programmed in them. They are incapable of giving any consideration to new developments that may bring into question, the resulting actions carried out by the contract.

The only other concern is that, whereas an on-chain feature might exist to allow verification of the source code of a smart contract, only a small subset of users might be in a position to truly understand it.

Conclusion

Smart contracts are decentralized applications, operating on blockchain technology. For this reason they benefit from some of the defining characteristics of the technology such as immutability and provenance.

Smart contracts are not direct digitization of legal contracts. Instead they are software implementations of rules of engagement between or among different parties. Whereas smart contracts preempt, or at the very least minimize contract disputes, they can still end up being the subject of litigation in a traditional court of law.

Finally, smart contracts are typically written for business, governments, NGOs and individuals by programmers, not lawyers, to serve a large group of entities in a standard, efficient and cost effective manner. The use cases for smart contracts are many, still growing and can only be limited by imagination.

The next chapter is about cryptocurrencies which are smart contracts, at least from a technical perspective.

Exercise 5

1. Briefly describe how smart contracts can be used in the Retail industry.

2. What are the benefits of using smart contracts for voting in elections?

3. List any other use cases for smart contracts, besides the ones mentioned in this chapter.

i. ______________________________

ii. ______________________________

iii. ______________________________

iv. ______________________________

v. ______________________________

Quiz 5

1 Complete the following statement.
The structure of a simple contract can be generalized as "if condition, then _________________".

a) no obligation(s)
b) terms
c) action(s)
d) condition(s)

2 Which of the following statements is **true**?

a) Smart contracts are duplicated on all the nodes of a blockchain.
b) Smart contracts can verify conditions, but do not carry out the action(s) for the prevailing condition.
c) Smart contracts do not verify conditions, but carry out the action(s) for the prevailing condition.
d) Smart contracts are duplicated on some of the nodes of a blockchain.

3 Which of the following statements **least describes** what a contract deployment transaction is?

a) It is a special transaction whose destination is specified as "0x0000000000000000000000000000000000000000".
b) It is the transaction executed to register a smart contract's EVM bytecode on a blockchain.
c) This is the transaction that sends the compiled code of a smart contract to the zero address to signify the registration of a new contract.
d) It is a special type of transaction for registering a new smart contract on a blockchain.

4 Which of the following statement is **false**?

a) The objective of contract law is to identify grievances and then resolve them.
b) Smart contracts are creative enough to see when some obligations are either unfair or unenforceable.

c) Smart contracts can minimize the need for contract litigation in certain scenarios.
d) The objective of smart contract is to act as an agent of the contracting parties and to actually carry out their obligations on their behalf.

5 Fill in the blanks.
A ______________ smart contract is one that requires information from outside its host blockchain to operate.
a) deterministic
b) oracle
c) ex ante
d) non-deterministic

6 Which of the following statements are **true**? (you may choose one or more)
i. All consumers have the competence and the required knowledge to influence smart contract operations.
ii. Oracles are necessary for non-deterministic smart contracts to improve their quality of decision making.
iii. In conformity with trustless systems, smart contracts, require trust between the parties, and external monitoring of contractual obligations or enforcement.
iv. Smart contracts are typically used in business transaction scenarios that target a large number of customers.
a) i only
b) iv only
c) ii and iv
d) i and iii

7 Complete the following statement.
In solidity, smart contract code is organized in units similar to ___________________________.
a) classes in procedural languages
b) methods in functions
c) classes in OOP languages
d) functions in OOP languages

8 Which of the following statements is **false**?

a) Smart contracts are similar to Standard Contract Forms.

b) Transactions sent to smart contract addresses may contain crypto, or data, or both, as parameters.

c) Smart contract generated transactions cannot change the state of the blockchain.

d) Decentralized Autonomous Organizations are special kinds of smart contacts.

9 Which of the following statements are **false**? (you may choose one or more)

i. Smart contracts lower the risk of collaboration.

ii. Smart contracts are trustless systems.

iii. Smart contracts unlike transactions on blockchains are not immutable.

iv. Smart contracts' functionality is predictable, transparent and independently verifiable.

a) ii only

b) ii and iii

c) iii only

d) i, ii and iii

10 Which of the following **best describes** a shortcoming of smart contracts?

a) Smart contracts are rigid.

b) Smart contracts are unable to give any consideration to new developments that designers/programmers had not taken into account.

c) Smart contracts are not smart.

d) Smart contracts cannot yet completely replace contract law and lawyers.

References

1 Hsueh, V. and Deylami, S. (2022). *1.6: Thomas Hobbes — Excerpts from Leviathan, 1651.* [online] Social Sci LibreTexts. Available at: https://socialsci.libretexts.org/Courses/Western_Washington_University/Introduction_to_Political_Theory_I/01%3A_Readings/1.06%3A_Thomas_Hobbes__Excerpts_from_Leviathan_1651 [Accessed 18 Jun. 2025].

2 Gans, J.S. (2021). The Fine Print in Smart Contracts. In: M.C. Compagnucci, M. Fenwick and S. Wrbka, eds., *Smart Contracts: Technological, Business and Legal Perspectives.* Oxford; New York: Hart Publishing, p. 57.

3 Gans, J.S. (2021). The Fine Print in Smart Contracts. In: M.C. Compagnucci, M. Fenwick and S. Wrbka, eds., *Smart Contracts: Technological, Business and Legal Perspectives.* Oxford; New York: Hart Publishing, pp. 39-40.

4 Szabo, N. (1994). *Smart Contracts.* [online] www.fon.hum.uva.nl. Available at: https://www.fon.hum.uva.nl/rob/Courses/InformationInSpeech/CDROM/Literature/LOTwinterschool2006/szabo.best.vwh.net/smart.contracts.html [Accessed 19 Jun. 2025].

5 Lacity, M.C. and Lupien, S.C. (2022). *Blockchain Fundamentals for Web 3.0.* University of Arkansas Press, pp.113, 114.

6 Ashurst, S. and Tempesta, S. (2022). *Blockchain applied : practical technology and use cases of enterprise blockchain for the real world.* Boca Raton, Florida: Routledge, pp.43, 48.

7 Crypto Dukedom (2021). *The Nft Revolution - Real Estate Edition.* Crypto Dukedom, p.30.

8 Compagnucci, M.C., Fenwick, M. and Wrbka, S. (2021). Introduction: The Technology, Use-Cases and Law of Smart Contracts. In: M.C. Compagnucci, M. Fenwick and S. Wrbka, eds., *Smart Contracts: Technological, Business and Legal Perspectives.* Oxford ; New York: Hart Publishing, p.1.

9 Werbach , K. and Cornell, N. (2021). Contracts: Ex Machina.

In: M.C. Compagnucci, M. Fenwick and S. Wrbka, eds., *Smart Contracts: Technological, Business and Legal Perspectives.* Oxford ; New York: Hart Publishing, pp.10,21, 9, 24, 25, 23,19.

10 Wrbka, S. (2021). A Multilayer Safeguard Mechanism. In: M.C. Compagnucci, M. Fenwick and S. Wrbka, eds., *Smart Contracts: Technological, Business and Legal Perspectives.* Oxford ; New York: Hart Publishing, pp.131, 128, 133,124.

11 Modi, R. (2022). *Solidity Programming Essentials.* 2nd ed. Packt Publishing Ltd, pp. 26, 62,191.

12 Infante, R. (2019). *Building Ethereum Dapps: Decentralized Applications on the Ethereum Blockchain.* Manning Incorporated, pp. 85, 171, 173.

13 Antonopoulos, A.M. and Wood Ph.D, G. (2018). *Mastering Ethereum.* O'Reilly Media, pp. 98, 102.

14 VOSS, W.G. (2021). Data Protection Issues for Smart Contracts. In: M.C. Compagnucci, M. Fenwick and S. Wrbka, eds., *Smart Contracts: Technological, Business and Legal Perspectives.* Oxford ; New York: Hart Publishing, p.79.

15 Vogelsteller , F. and Terbu, O. (2021). Identity in the Ethereum blockchain ecosystem. In: *Self-Sovereign Identity: DECENTRALIZED DIGITAL IDENTITY AND VERIFIABLE CREDENTIALS* . Shelter Island, NY 11964: Manning Publications Co., pp.425–426.

16 Ashurst, S. and Tempesta, S. (2022). *Blockchain applied : practical technology and use cases of enterprise blockchain for the real world.* Boca Raton, Florida: Routledge, pp.36-37.

17 Fortnow, M. and Terry, Q. (2021). *NFT HANDBOOK : how to create, sell and buy non -fungible tokens.* S.L.: John Wiley, p.162.

18 Infante, R. (2019). *Building Ethereum Dapps: Decentralized Applications on the Ethereum Blockchain.* Manning Incorporated, pp. 57-58.

6. Cryptocurrencies

"Crypto is not just about making money; it's about changing the world by democratizing finance and giving power back to the people"
- Andreas M. Antonopoulos

6.1 Introduction

Currency is standardized money in the form of bank notes and/or coins used in a particular jurisdiction. The jurisdiction is usually a single country; however, there are cases where a group of countries have an agreement to use the same currency. This is the case for the European Union, where member states use the Euro. A key thing to note is that there is usually an authority that decides what currency will be used in the area under its control[1].

Modern currency is a solution to the problems presented by barter trade, which are best illustrated by examples.

Supposing Tom has some cabbage that he doesn't need and he specifically wants goat meat in exchange. He could go to the market with his cabbage, expecting to find someone who will give him goat meat. The first problem is that, on that day, Tom might find no one with goat meat. Secondly, Tom might find someone with goat meat, but with no interest in his cabbage. Thirdly, Tom may find a person who wants his cabbage, but has something else, such as eggs, rather than goat meat. Lastly, assuming that Tom finds someone with goat meat and wants cabbage, should the person really accept to exchange a whole goat for a cabbage ? Are they of the same value ? Suffice it to say that with barter trade, a "double coincidence of wants", is hard to come by.

A work around for the above problems is to use a middleman, but it would at the very least, cost a portion of the goods being exchanged, such that the trading partners end up with less of whatever was due to them. In some cases, a significant amount of time might elapse before traders get what they want. This is unacceptable, especially for perishable goods.

A better solution is to use an item that most traders would accept for most goods. At some point in history, such an item was cowry shells. This is what is referred to as a "**means of exchange**". The means of exchange should be divisible to facilitate purchase of goods of varying sizes e.g. a kilo of goat meat, or a whole goat. In other words, the means of exchange should have "**units of account**". So, suppose Tom goes to the market but does not find goat meat, but manages to gets someone willing to take his cabbages. It makes sense for Tom to release the cabbages to this person before they go bad and accept "Cowry shells". Suppose Tom receives two "Cowry shells" for his two cabbages, and on that day, this would have afforded him, one quarter of a kilo of goat meat. It should be that, if Tom were to return to the market three or more days or weeks later, the two "Cowry shells" should still be enough to afford him a quarter of a kilo of goat meat. In other words, the value of a means of exchange should be relatively stable over time, or rather; a means of exchange should be "**a store of value**" for later purchases. Finally, a means of exchange ought to be **scarce** enough such that it is not easily obtained without cost e.g. labor. At the same time, it should not be so scarce, that it becomes unavailable when needed.

Later on, precious metals like silver and gold were used as a means of exchange. But because they were bulky, society started depositing them with merchants who would issue receipts for the metals. As time progressed, people started exchanging the receipts rather than the metals themselves. These precious metal receipts are the origin of today's currencies. However, unlike these deposit receipts that represented the existence and ownership of actual precious metal deposits, most modern fiat currencies are not backed by anything of value. Governments just print them, taking advantage of the psychological & coercive power that they have over the people in their jurisdiction, to give an illusion of value. In this sense then, currency is what people have accepted to serve as a means of exchange, acts as a store of value and has units of account[2].

6.2 A Brief History of Digital Currency

Digital currency is also referred to as virtual money or electronic currency.

Unbeknownst to many people digital money's originates as far back as the late 1980s, when a group of activists, technologists, and cryptographers known as Cypherpunks, advocated for its design and use. Cypherpunks argued that whereas cash offered anonymity to individuals, it was bulky, printed by governments and held in banks. Cypherpunks therefore envisioned "anonymous transaction systems", entirely out of the control of governments and big corporations like banks. Apart from this, the virtual currency had to exist solely on computers, with no physical representation. This, the Cypherpunks argued, would be democratic because the virtual currency would be under the control of its users[3].

Shortly after, in 1990, David Chaum launched ECash, the first cryptocurrency. One major drawback of ECash was that it was a centralized system, and so the company operating it,

DigiCash, was responsible for validating transactions. This portends a single point of failure[4].

Ultimately ECash did not succeed and so later on, other virtual currencies such as B-Money, Bit Gold and Hashcash came up to try where ECash had failed. Unfortunately, at the time, the market did not view these virtual currencies as improvements over cash or debit/credit cards[5].

First forward to the year 2008, and a person, or group of people going by the pseudo name Satoshi Nakamoto, created Bitcoin and shared about it at an online forum, through a whitepaper titled "Bitcoin: A Peer-to-Peer Electronic Cash System". The creator(s) preferred to remain anonymous. However, from the presentation, it was evident that the creator(s) had a high level of proficiency in a number of fields, hence the suspicion that it could be a group's work, and not that of a single person. Subsequently, Satoshi shared a prototype of Bitcoin in February 2009 and the journey of bitcoin and blockchain technology began in earnest[6].

The primary technology behind Bitcoin is blockchain. Blockchain technology itself heavily relies on cryptography. If you consider that Bitcoin facilitates peer to peer payments (read money or currency), then you already understand where the term cryptocurrency emanates from.

6.3 bitcoin

Notice that the title for this section begins with a lower case letter 'b'. This is not an error. Bitcoin starting with an upper case i.e. 'B' refers to the blockchain network or platform, while bitcoin with lower case letter i.e. 'b', is the cryptocurrency riding atop of it.

Prior to Bitcoin, individuals had not been able to send information securely over an unsecured network without the requirement of a trusted third party[7]. Now, using Public Key cryptography on a decentralized peer to peer network, this has become possible. It may surprise the reader to know that communications and transaction data are not protected on the network. Cryptography is used for authentication i.e. to verify the source of a transaction. And even after a transaction is deemed authentic, it still has to be validated before being written on to the ledger. Once accepted on to the ledger, cryptography is used for integrity preservation[8].

But what exactly is bitcoin? It is programmable money, a smart contract that has functions for crediting and debiting user balances. Furthermore, it can validate transactions to ensure a stable state for the network. For example, if Jane is paying out money, her balance must be more than the amount she is paying out, by at least the transaction fee amount. Also, the resulting balance after transaction must be less by the transaction amount and transaction fee. Using Jane's public key, a function will authenticate the transaction which Jane is expected to have signed with her private. The smart contract will also generate necessary success and error messages.

From the preceding paragraph, we can say that in blockchain networks, transactions do not carry digital currency. Instead they carry data about transactions such as whether it a credit or debit, originating address, destination address, transaction amount and digital signature. So in essence Bitcoin is an immutable, append only, digital distributed ledger that tracks account balances by logging debit and credit transactions of bitcoin[9].

At this point, a good question would be "if currency does not move around from one account to another, what are wallets for?".

6.4 Digital Wallets

Technically, digital wallets are not for storing cryptos (cryptocurrency). A wallet is actually software for generating, storing and managing a user's public-private key pairs and sending transaction requests[10].

The public key is used to generate a wallet address. A wallet address is like a bank account number. Once a transaction is made transferring crypto to a newly created wallet address, the only authentic transactions that can move crypto out of that account are those signed by the private key that was generated together with the public key that generated the wallet address (account) .

If you have not got it yet, then understand that whoever knows your private key can make transactions to move cryptocurrency out of your account and sign them using your private key. There is one more danger. If you yourself lose your private key(s) i.e. cannot access it because it is misplaced, deleted or corrupted, then your coins are lost for good. Now you know why private keys have to be guarded jealously. There are several ways of storing private keys[11]:

i) Using the wallet application installed locally on your computer or smart phone that was used to generate the key pairs. If your device is frequently connected to the internet, then there is a risk that it could be hacked and your private keys stolen remotely. So, one of the things you should ensure is that your private keys are encrypted before storage.

ii) Online wallets are installed on some server computer that is always connected to the internet. This could be on an exchange where cryptocurrencies are traded or on a server operated by an organization providing Software as a service (SaaS). Either way, the fact that it is always online implies that it could be hacked. Apart from this, it is possible in some cases, that the employees of the organization hosting the wallets could gain access to your private keys and thus steal cryptocurrency from your account. This is therefore the least safe wallet.

iii) Hardware wallets are special devices designed to store private keys in an encrypted form, thus making it difficult to decipher the plain text value of private keys. They are only connected to a device when necessary, but at all other times, they are offline. Normally the designers of hardware wallets make use of open source software so that customers can verify the integrity of the software being used to handle the security of their private keys. Since hardware wallets are comparatively the most secure, they are also the most expensive option.

iv) Paper wallets are yet another way of storing your private keys offline. You could either print it or write it on a piece of paper and then store it somewhere securely from people and elements like water and fire.

It is possible, and actually recommended in some cases, that an individual uses several different accounts for cryptocurrencies to avoid being monitored. For example, if you purchase an item using your bitcoin account, nothing would stop the seller from using the Bitcoin explorer to track your transactions using your wallet address. The reverse is also true. Nothing stops you as well, from tracking the seller's transactions using the wallet address that they provided for payment. If this upsets you, remember that transparency is one of benefits of collaboration on blockchain networks.

6.5 bitcoin Mining

When discussing means of exchange or money in the Introduction section, it was mentioned that one of its properties is that it should be scarce. To introduce the element of scarcity for bitcoin, its maximum supply was capped at 21 million bitcoins. This is unlike fiat currency that governments print at will, thus devaluing currency and driving up the cost of living.

The maximum supply of bitcoins was not released in one go. Instead, from 2009 up to now, Bitcoin network has ensured a mathematically metered supply of bitcoins through mining and the **coinbase transaction**.

This works as follows. Approximately every 10 minutes, a new block is accepted on to the chain, and on this block, the system appends a special bitcoin transaction which is a payment to the node whose block has been accepted onto the chain. It is this system generated transaction that introduces new bitcoins into the network that is called the coinbase transaction[13].

In order for a node to get its block accepted, it has to engage in a process called mining. In this process, mining nodes collect new bitcoin transactions being broadcast across the network. Once the transactions have accumulated to a predefined block size, the nodes have to do some mathematical computations (cryptographic) to find a special number called a "**nonce**", which when used together with other inputs, generates a specific hash for the current block. The correct nonce can only be found by brute force computation i.e. trial and error. This implies repeatedly trying a different nonce value until the requirement is met. For example the requirement could be that the hash of the current block should start with 30 zeros. Once a mining node finds the correct solution, it broadcasts this solution to other nodes to verify. This is what is called **proof of work** (PoW)[14].

As soon as the other nodes are aware that the correct solution has been found, they stop seeking a solution for the current block, accept the new block and begin seeking a solution for the next block. Meanwhile the node that found the solution is paid some bitcoin for successful mining through the coinbase transaction. In other words, some new bitcoins have been minted i.e. introduced into the network.

Note that mining operations are not productive in any way, apart from helping to space out the interval between which new blocks are appended on to the chain. So miners are paid primarily for maintaining a ledger whose contents are determined through the network's consensus mechanism and for validating transactions. So they help safeguard the integrity of the network.

It costs a lot of money to engage in mining operations. Whereas in the beginning mining could be carried out using normal computer Central Processing Units (CPUs), operators soon realized that they could solve the cryptographic puzzle faster, if they used a Graphics Processing Unit (GPU) attached to a computer. This meant they could mint more crypto for themselves. And so the race, or greed, began in earnest, and people started using GPU rigs i.e. a group of GPUs coupled together for faster computation. Figure 6.1 shows what a mining rig looks like. CPU miners no longer had much of a chance to mint bitcoin.

Figure 6.1 GPU Mining Rig[17]

From GPU rigs, financially able miners moved to Application Specific Integrated Circuits (ASICs). Unlike GPU rigs which are comparatively bulky, and assembled on a rack by the miner himself or herself, ASICs are factory made specifically for crypto mining and are by far much more powerful. Figure 6.2 shows what an ASIC device looks like.

Figure 6.2 ASIC Device [18]

To compound the problem for the financially less endowed miners, individuals and corporations started creating mining farms using ASICs. Essentially, it is a setup where a very large number of ASICs are coupled to work together for much faster computation than is possible with mining rigs. Figure 6.3 shows what an ASIC mining farm looks like.

Figure 6.3: ASIC Mining Farm[19]

One problem with the mining farm approach is that it is likely to require site rentals. Additional personnel will also be required for security and operational maintenance. Apart from that, the utility bills especially, for electricity is also very high. The mining equipment generates a lot of heat, which necessitates cooling. Cooling also requires electricity.

To put things into perspective, US Energy Information Administration in a publication released in 2024, estimated that energy consumed by cryptocurrency mining is in the range of 0.6% to 2.3% of the total U.S. electricity consumption[20]. About seven years prior to that, the Guardian reported that energy consumption from Bitcoin's mining alone used more electricity per year, than the whole of Ireland[21]. For this reason, some mining farms are situated in cold places in order to realize lower cooling costs.

So, miners are also paid in bitcoin to compensate them for their investment in hardware devices which they use to help safeguard the integrity of the network. They are also paid for their operational costs such as rent, electricity and personnel.

Currently, the value of the block reward is 3.125 bitcoins plus transaction fees. This bitcoin amount translates to about USD 372,384.69. The transaction fee fluctuates widely, and is dependent on transaction amounts. By 22 July 2025, for the same month, the transaction fee ranged between US$ 0.8995 and 1.752.

Note: The block reward has not always been the same as it is currently. It was initially 50 bitcoins in 2009; however, the system was configured to halve this value approximately every four years. So it as moved from 50 to 25, to 12.5, to 6.25, and currently 3.125.

If you consider that the current value of one bitcoin translates to about USD 118,963.00, then you will probably agree that most bitcoin transaction amounts are likely to be under 1 bitcoin e.g. 0.000005btc. Unlike other cryptos, bitcoin has only two denominations i.e. bitcoin itself and satoshis. There are 100, 000, 000 satoshis in one bitcoin. So as time goes by, it is increasingly convenient to mention transaction amounts in satoshis rather than bitcoin. For example instead of saying 0.000005 BTC, we talk of 5 thousand satoshis[22].

Recall that for public blockchains, miners are free to join or quit the network arbitrarily. The import of this is that the computing power available over the entire network, otherwise known as the **Total Hash Rate**, varies over time and this affects the frequency of generating new blocks. To maintain a steady frequency of block generation to about one block every 10 minutes, the blockchain system adjusts a certain variable called the **Difficulty**, based on the time it took to mine the last 2016 blocks i.e. approximately every two weeks. The Difficulty is recalculated as follows[15].

$$\text{New Difficulty Target} = \text{Old Difficulty Target} \times (\text{Time Taken for Last 2016 Blocks} / 1209600 \text{ seconds})$$

Suffice it to say that bitcoins scarcity is maintained through mining activity, whose difficulty is varied based on the networks total hash rate, to ensure a near constant interval before subsequent supply.

6.6 Altcoins

Bitcoin remains the "most visible, on-going, live experiment for an open, public, secure, non-governmental, and non-TTP reliant application"[23]. Its use cases include person to person remittances, international business payments as well as e-commerce. However, a key drawback of Bitcoin was that it was designed to solve only one problem, which is money transfer. It has no other use cases particularly within enterprise environments.

Techies soon noticed other limitations that they could improve upon such as data storage, functionality, and settlement times. So because Bitcoin is open source, they downloaded the software and made alterations to the program code. In most cases, early modifications resulted in alternative coins to bitcoin, hence the origin of the term "Altcoins". Two examples of altcoins that were launched in 2011 are Litecoin (LTC) and Namecoin (NMC)[24].

To fix the problem of limited applicability especially in the enterprise world, general purpose blockchain networks such as Ethereum were developed and launched. Typically such have their own native cryptocurrency, but allow the development of other currencies by non-core developers of the underlying blockchain network. The number of cryptocurrencies exploded.

At the time of writing this section in July 2025, there are 18,815 cryptocurrencies which is slightly over 100 times more than the fiat currencies in the world. The combined value of cryptos in circulation, or the global crypto market cap, according to CoinMarketCap is US$3.77T. If you consider that blockchain technology is still developing, then this number will only continue to grow[25].

Nevertheless, to determine the value of a cryptocurrency, one has to look at how the underlying network is used. If it solves significant problem(s) for a large section of the society, then this could have a positive impact on the value of the cryptocurrency. This is called **utility value**. Otherwise, some currencies only have a **speculative value** i.e. a large number of people just buy them in hope that its value will increase and then they sell it at a profit. In many cases, newly launched, cryptocurrencies are bought based on their speculative value from advertising before the use of the network picks up. The speculative value might be informed by the belief that due to the utility value, the demand for the product will rise. However, if they have no actual utility value, prices will be unstable and demand will ultimately plummet.

In their book "CryptoAssets", Chris Burniske and Jack Tatar suggest a number of ways of applying fundamental analysis before buying cryptos. This includes reading the white paper, examining the issuance model, learning about the community behind the crypto (including its developers) and also comparing the candidate cryptos to other similar ones before them. They further suggest that the number of exchanges that support a crypto is an indicator of acceptance. In such cases, one can examine the volume of trades with dominant cryptos like bitcoin. An even deeper evidence of acceptance and thus demand, is when a crypto is supported by regulated exchanges, and has a significant number of trading pairs with dominant fiat currencies[24].

In the rest of this section, we will have a brief look at a few other cryptocurrencies.

Note: The fact that a cryptocurrency is mentioned in this book does not equate to advice to purchase any of them. Do your own due diligence.

Ethereum

You have already encountered Ethereum when learning about smart contracts. As a quick recap, Ethereum is a general purpose programmable blockchain, so it has diverse implementations running on it including different cryptocurrencies by different communities.

However, Ethereum has its own native currency called **Ether** (symbol is ETH). Ether is primarily used to pay for Gas, which is used to limit resource usage on the network to forestall denial of service attacks. In other words, without charging for transactions or computational costs, some programs might be written in a manner that they end up running in an indefinite loop, thus denying other programs in the network, access to resources. So on Ethereum network, different types of transactions have different Gas costs that fluctuate based on network demand. As soon as the Gas cost that was paid in Ether runs out, the program terminates automatically. This means that it would cost a malicious attacker dearly, if he or she wanted to monopolize resources on the network[26].

In 2016, there was a security breach on a smart contract known as The DAO that led to the loss of a large amount of cryptocurrency. Subsequently, there was a disagreement in the community on how to resolve the issue of the lost crypto. Whereas one group wanted the stolen crypto to be reversed, the other group viewed this action as contrary to the principle of immutability of blockchains. This led to an Ethereum fork that resulted in two competing coins. So now there is Ethereum (ETH), supported by the first group and Ethereum Classic (ETC), supported by the dissenters. Ethereum (ETH) has fared much better than Ethereum Classic (ETC) in terms of demand and pricing.

Ether has 5 denominations, with Ether itself being the biggest and Wei being the smallest. Table 6.1 summarizes their relationships with respect to Wei.

Unit	Ether	ETH Value	Wei	Wei Value
Wei	0.000000000000000001	1e-18 ETH	1	1 Wei
Kwei (Babbage)	0.000000000000001	1e-15 ETH	1,000	1e3 Wei
Mwei (Lovelace)	0.000000000001	1e-12 ETH	1,000,000	1e6 Wei
Gwei (Shannon)	0.000000001	1e-9 ETH	1,000,000,000	1e9 Wei
Microether (Szabo)	0.000001	1e-6 ETH	1,000,000,000,000	1e12 Wei
Milliether (Finney)	0.001	1e-3 ETH	1,000,000,000,000,000	1e15 Wei
Ether	1	1 ETH	1,000,000,000,000,000,000	1e18 Wei

Table 6.1: Ether denominations

For example, 1 Gwei (from Gigawei) is equivalent to 1,000,000,000 Wei and 1 Ether is equivalent to 1,000,000,000,000,000,000 Wei. Apart from Ether and Wei, all the other denominations were given an alternative name as a tribute to pioneer contributors in the digital money industry. For example Shannon (Gwei) is in honor of the father of Information Theory, Claude Shannon (Mathematician/Cryptographer). Wei itself is named after the inventor of B-money, who is called Wei Dai[27].

Ripple

Ripple is the product of a privately owned company, also called Ripple. Its symbol is XRP and it operates on a blockchain network called XRP Ledger (XRPL). One of the advantages that Ripple has, is that it can be integrated with both decentralized blockchain applications as well as the traditional ones.

Ripples main use case is near real time gross settlement of funds between any two places in the world. It does this by acting as a bridge between not just to fiat currencies, but "any unit that has value like frequent flier miles, virtual currencies, and mobile minutes"[28]. For example, consider money transfer of dollars, from a sender in New York, USA to a recipient in Tokyo, Japan. The spot price of USD/XRP is determined at the sender's bank and then used to transfer an equivalent amount of XRPs. At the receiving end, the spot price of XRP/YEN is used to determine the amount of Japanese Yen to deposit in the recipient's account. This transfer takes approximately only 4 seconds and is thus not heavily impacted by price fluctuations. Other than that, the transaction costs are negligible, making it suitable for micro payment business models as well.

From this example one can infer, that Ripple requires a network of banks, payment providers, and digital asset exchanges to in order to transfer money globally. Indeed, through its product RippleNet, Ripple has managed to achieve about 95% of market share, including over 200 banks around the world.

Ripple is different from other cryptocurrencies in at least two significant ways. The first one is that all the 100 billion XRPs in circulation were pre-mined from the onset. Unlike other cryptocurrencies, mining is not an ongoing exercise. Secondly, at any given time, only a subset of the nodes on the network participates in the exercise of validating transactions. This makes the RippleNet much faster than bitcoin and Ethereum. It can even be scaled so that its throughput (transactions per second) matches that of VISA.

Ripple has another similar product called Stellar, that targets individuals rather than financial institutions. However, in comparison to Ripple, its adoption is not as widespread by a big margin.

Currently Ripple/XRP stands third among cryptocurrencies in terms of value, with a market capitalization of slightly above $188.01 billion. As more individuals & businesses get a better understanding of blockchain technology, a fast, transparent, efficient and inexpensive micropayment system such as Ripple/XRP can only expect further widespread adoption[29].

6.7 Stablecoins

Stablecoins are a type of cryptocurrency that are collateralized to existing assets outside the blockchain networks that hosts them. This is similar to the time when currencies were actually backed by valuable minerals such as gold. For example, a $10 bill by a specific issuer implied that the issuer had in his reserve, gold worth $10 and that, if the bearer presented the $10 bill to the issuer, the issuer was obligated to give him/her gold for that amount.

Likewise stablecoins are deemed stable because of the collateral item that it is based on. It is expected that if you present a stablecoin to the issuer, he should be in the position to give you the collateral that backs it. Other than that, the collateral has a price stabilizing effect on the stablecoin because their price does not fluctuate as widely as that of other cryptocurrencies. So reference to stability here is made only in relative terms. Stablecoins are fungible meaning that a unit of a given stable coin can be swapped with another unit of the same stable coin, without resulting in loss of value[30].

Whereas most stable coins are **fiat-collateralized**, they can also be backed by other items such as commodities and even cryptocurrency. Commodities include precious metals like gold, silver and diamonds. They may also include other collaterals of value like crude oil or grains. An example of **commodity-collateralized** stablecoin is Digix Gold (DGX).

Stablecoins backed by fiat currency are authoritative because the asset they are pegged on is issued by government. Pegging in this context implies a fixed conversion rate to or from a fiat currency or commodity money. A leading example of fiat-collateralized stablecoin is USDt issued by Tether Limited Inc. From its symbol one can infer that it is pegged to the USD. However, lately Tether Limited Inc have also put into circulation, additional tokens that represent the Euro (EURt), Chinese Yuan (CNHt), Mexican Pesso (MXNt) and Gold (XAUt). In terms of value among cryptocurrencies, USDt is currently fourth behind Ripple/XRP, with a market cap of about US$ 163.58 Billion. Another fiat currency backed stablecoin is USDc, issued by Circle. USDc currently sits seventh among all cryptocurrencies in terms of market value and has a market cap of $63.86 Billion.

There are also stablecoins which are backed by another cryptocurrency instead of fiat currency. This type of stablecoin is said to be **crypto-collateralized.** One example is Wrapped Bitcoin (WBTC) which is issued on the Ethereum blockchain. Another is MakerDAO (DAI). Stablecoins backed by cryptocurrency are likely to mirror the price volatility of the asset backing it [31, 32, 25].

Yet another category of stablecoins is **algorithmic stablecoins.** Their key characteristic is that they are not backed by any collateral. Instead, they employ computer algorithms (smart contracts) to manage the supply of the currency in response to market demands. Their key selling points are scalability and auditability. Since they are not limited by physical assets, their supply can easily be increased. And because they are purely on-chain, they are easy to audit[33].

The primary use case for stablecoins is to facilitate trading across different cryptocurrency exchanges. In this case, they eliminate the necessity to convert one cryptocurrency to fiat currency before purchasing another cryptocurrency, thus saving on transaction costs and time.

However, stablecoins have a few disadvantages. The first concern is that stablecoin issuance is organized in a centralized manner. This creates some mistrust because central authorities tend to abuse their power. Secondly, many financial institutions are coming up with their own stablecoins that are not necessarily exchangeable with that of their counterparts. So the stablecoin that one holds matters. It should be noted that Ripple/XRP already appears to have solved the problem that many of these institutions are trying to solve with their individual stablecoins. Thirdly, stablecoins issuing institutions ought to be audited regularly for the assurance that they indeed have the advertised collateral for their coins. Lastly, most stablecoin issuers are private organizations and therefore they may not necessarily share their code or their Applications Programming Interface (APIs)[30, 31].

6.8 Privacy Coins

Recall that earlier in this chapter, it was mentioned that ordinarily cryptocurrency transactions on a blockchain are transparent, such that once a wallet address is known, it can be monitored. Whereas it is true that wallet addresses do not bare names, it may be possible, over time, through the use of algorithms to discover the true identities of transacting parties.

It is for this reason that wallet addresses on networks like Bitcoin are considered 'pseudoanonymous'[34]. This lack of complete privacy is undesirable for some people and so privacy coins emerged as a solution to this problem.

Monero (XMR) is an example of a privacy protecting cryptocurrency. It operates on its own blockchain network. At the time of this writing, it sits 25th among all cryptocurrencies in terms of value, with a market cap of US$ 5.77B.

Monero employs ring signatures to solve the privacy problem. Like with other cryptocurrencies, individuals with Monero wallets have a private and a public key. However, with Monero, once an initiator has signed a transaction and it has been broadcast on the network, the system randomly selects a number of signatures that were used for past transactions and adds them as additional signatures to the current transaction output. These extra signatures act as decoys making it difficult to determine the originator of the transaction[35].

Another difference between Monero and other cryptocurrency blockchains is that its PoW algorithm is ASIC resistant. In other words, the algorithm favors the use of CPUs or GPUs over ASICs for mining, therefore making it more inclusive for ordinary folk[36].

Other examples of privacy coins are Worldcoin, Immutable, PancakeSwap and Zcash. All of these currently have a market cap exceeding US$ 500 million, which is testament to the fact that there is an interest and a market for privacy coins[37].

Predictably, the main concern regarding privacy coins is that they could be used to facilitate illegal activities such as funding terrorism, drug trafficking, or money laundering.

6.9 Central Bank Digital Currencies (CBDCs)

Central Bank Digital Currencies (CBDCs) are just digital currencies issued by a central bank. As one would expect, CBDCs are not decentralized. One could view them as government issued stablecoins backed by the national fiat currency.

The primary reason some governments are working towards operating CBCDs is cryptophobia i.e. fear of competition from private digital currencies. However, the reason offered is that CBCDs would streamline international trade finance and reduce dependency on the dollar. In 2020, the Bank for International Settlements produced a joint paper on CBDCs advocating for its use. The other contributors were Bank of Canada, European Central Bank, Bank of Japan, Sveriges Riksbank, Swiss National Bank, Bank of England and Board of Governors Federal Reserve System. By 2025, countries like China, India, Brazil, Nigeria, Japan, Australia, Sweden, United States, United Kingdom and the European Union had started working towards implementation of CBDCs[38, 39].

The idea of a CBDC has not been received very well by private, freedom loving citizens, because governments can use them in many unfavorable ways against their citizens. CBDCs are fully programmable and centralized, so rogue governments can control when, where and how much is spent by any individual. Furthermore, tyrannical governments can determine what you can or cannot spend your money on.

Any government that has total control of your finances and assets can consequently control your behavior as well. So CBDCs can be used to punish dissent, and to enforce unpopular mandates such as vaccinations. Lastly CBDCs can be used by elements in governments to facilitate surveillance capitalism where they collect personal financial data for individuals and sell it to corporate organizations.

6.10 Crypto Exchanges

Crypto exchanges provide a convenient platform for individuals to buy and sell crypto. To participate, one must have a wallet (private keys included) under the control of the exchange. The implication of this arrangement is that it brings back the element of centrality and middleman (Trusted Third Party). This is the origin of the term Centralized-Decentralized Finance (CeDeFi). CeDeFi is against what the original adopters of cryptocurrency envisaged. Nevertheless, many people prefer to have an exchange manage their wallets on their behalf. But this comes at a cost.

Crypto exchanges at the very least, charge their customers for each transaction on their platform. Apart from this, they are government regulated. This is primarily to forestall the possibility of the exchange owners disappearing with customers' money. As a prerequisite for licensing, they are expected to comply with Know Your Customer (KYC) and anti-money laundering (AML) requirements. This throws anonymity of the customer out through the window and makes it easier for predatory taxation and monitoring by government[40].

At the time of writing this section, CoinMarketCap lists 834 Crypto exchanges. The leading one is Binance with a daily trading volume of about US$ 21.6 Billion. Others in the top five include ByBit, Coinbase Exchange, Upbit and OKX[41]. Whereas most Crypto exchanges are likely to be stationed and regulated from the United States or some part of Europe, they typically serve customers from any part of the world, that have connection to the internet.

Conclusion

Cryptocurrencies are a new asset class that offers great opportunity for those who invest in them, but more so for private innovators who can come up with use cases that will drive up demand for their coins.

Programmable money under the control of tyrants will be any citizen's nightmare. But the greatest concern for an investor regarding cryptocurrencies and any digital assets for that matter, is, what happens if one day for some reason, electricity or even the internet itself, was unavailable over entire regions, or even the whole world, for days, maybe weeks, maybe for the foreseeable future ? This is unlikely, but still, a real possibility.

Exercise 6

1. Briefly describe an ICO (Initial Coin Offering).

2. Briefly describe IPO (Initial Public Offering).

3. List five differences between an IPO and an ICO.

   i.

ii.

iii.

iv.

v.

Quiz 6

1 Complete the following statement.
A means of exchange should have ________________.
a) plenty of denominations
b) decreasing store of value
c) some complexity
d) units of account

2 Which of the following statements about digital money is **true**?
a) The very first cryptocurrency is bitcoin.
b) The idea of digital money was first introduced by Satoshi Nakamoto.
c) The idea of digital money was originated by Cypherpunks.
d) The primary technology behind Blockchain is Bitcoin.

3 Which of the following statements are **false**? (you may choose one or more)
i. Communications and transaction data is cryptographically protected on the Bitcoin network.
ii. The existence of bitcoin is only supported by transactions and addresses.
iii. Bitcoin with capital 'B' refers to the cryptocurrency, while bitcoin with lower case 'b', is the platform.
iv. Technically, in cryptocurrency blockchains, transactions carry debit and credit data, not digital currency.
a) i and iii
b) i, ii and iv
c) iii only
d) None of the above

4 Which of the following is **not true** about crypto currency wallets?
a) A wallet address is generated from a private key.
b) A wallet address is akin to a bank account number.

c) Options for storing private keys include paper wallets.
d) The public key is used to generate a wallet address.

5 Which of the following statements **best describes** mining with respect to bitcoin?
a) Mining is the process of finding the nonce, which when used together with other inputs, generates the required hash for the current block.
b) Mining is the Bitcoin networks way of determining who to pay for transaction validations.
c) Mining is the activity used to regulate the supply of bitcoin into the network.
d) Mining is an activity mostly carried out in mining farms using ASICs.

6 Which of the following statements is **false**?
a) Bitcoin equals software, while bitcoin equals currency.
b) Bitcoin software code is proprietary and cannot be downloaded for modification.
c) Bitcoin was designed primarily to solve the problem of money transfer in unsecure networks.
d) Mining using CPUs was hugely profitable in 2009.

7 Which of the following **best describes** stablecoins?
a) Stablecoins can be backed by fiat currency, commodities, cryptocurrency or by no collateral at all.
b) Stablecoins are a type of cryptocurrency that are pegged to existing assets outside the blockchain networks that hosts them.
c) Stablecoins are fungible.
d) Stablecoins are used to facilitate trading across different cryptocurrency exchanges.

8 Which of the following statements are **true** regarding ICOs? (you may choose one or more)

i. Prior to an ICO, the concerned startup is required to register with a government regulatory agency.
ii. Coins issued at an ICO are traded at cryptocurrency exchanges, which are not all subject to regulation.
iii. Prior to an ICO, startup founders are not always subjected to thorough background checks.
iv. After an ICO, a startup is required to provide financial statements as well as business updates to the public investors.

a) i and ii
b) ii and iv
c) ii and iii
d) None of the above

9 Fill in the blanks.
Monero employs ________________ to solve the privacy problem.

a) digital signatures
b) privacy coins
c) stablecoins
d) ring signatures

10 Which of the following statements **least describes** CBDCs?

a) CBDCs are fungible digital coins.
b) CBDCs are digital currencies issued by a central bank.
c) CBDCs are conceptually like government issued stablecoins backed by the national fiat currency.
d) CBDCs are fully programmable and centralized digital currencies issued, and controlled by government agencies.

References

1 Wikipedia Contributors (2019). *Currency*. [online] Wikipedia. Available at: https://en.wikipedia.org/wiki/Currency [Accessed 7 Jul. 2025].

2 Burniske, C. and Tatar, J. (2018). *Cryptoassets : : The Innovative Investor's Guide to Bitcoin and Beyond /*. New York, N.Y.: Mcgraw-Hill Education, p.99.

3 Magnuson, W.J. (2020). *Blockchain democracy : technology, law and the rule of the crowd*. Cambridge, United Kingdom ; New York, Ny, Usa: Cambridge University Press, pp.25- 27.

4 Lacity, M.C. and Lupien, S.C. (2022). *Blockchain Fundamentals for Web 3.0*. University of Arkansas Press, p.136.

5 Magnuson, W.J. (2020b). *Blockchain democracy : technology, law and the rule of the crowd*. Cambridge, United Kingdom ; New York, Ny, Usa: Cambridge University Press, p.30.

6 Pritzker, Y. (2019). *Inventing bitcoin : the technology behind the first truly scarce and decentralized money explained*. United States, p.3.

7 Kelly, B. (2015). *The bitcoin big bang : how alternative currencies are about to change the world*. Hoboken, New Jersey: Wiley, p.140.

8 Antonopoulos, A.M. and Wood Ph.D, G. (2018). *Mastering Ethereum*. O'Reilly Media, p. 55.

9 Infante, R. (2019). *Building Ethereum Dapps: Decentralized Applications on the Ethereum Blockchain*. Manning Incorporated, p. 93.

10 Ashurst, S. and Tempesta, S. (2022). *Blockchain applied : practical technology and use cases of enterprise blockchain for the real world*. Boca Raton, Florida: Routledge, p.30.

11 Hellwig, D., Karlic , G. and Huchzermeier, A. (2020). *Build Your Own Blockchain*. Switzerland: Springer International Publishing, pp.43–45.

12 Nakamoto, S. (2008). *Bitcoin: a Peer-to-Peer Electronic Cash System*. [online] *bitcoin.org*. Available at: https://bitcoin.org/bitcoin.pdf [Accessed 14 Jul. 2025].

13 Burniske, C. and Tatar, J. (2018). *Cryptoassets : : The Innovative*

Investor's Guide to Bitcoin and Beyond /. New York, N.Y.: Mcgraw-Hill Education, p.105.

14 Ashurst, S. and Tempesta, S. (2022). *Blockchain applied : practical technology and use cases of enterprise blockchain for the real world.* Boca Raton, Florida: Routledge, p.26.

15 Bitcoin.com (2025). *What Is Difficulty Adjustment? | Bitcoin.com.* [online] Bitcoin.com. Available at: https://markets.bitcoin.com/glossary/difficulty-adjustment [Accessed 16 Jul. 2025].

16 Sun, W., Wu, X. (Brian) and Kwok, A. (2019). *Security Tokens and Stablecoins Quick Start Guide : Learn How to Build STO and Stablecoin Decentralized Applications.* Birmingham: Packt Publishing, Limited, pp.45-46.

17 ubuy (2025). *Solid Steel 8 GPU Open Air Mining Rig Frame.* [online] Ubuy Kenya. Available at: https://www.ubuy.ke/en/product/BSGJIU8-steel-open-air-miner-mining-frame-rig-case-mining-rig-frame-up-to-8-gpu-for-crypto-coin-currency-bitcoin-mining-accessories-tools-frame-only-fans-gpu [Accessed 18 Jul. 2025].

18 RigsMineria (2023). *Cryptocurrency mines.* [online] Rigs Minería. Available at: https://www.rigsmineria.com/en/cryptocurrency-mines/ [Accessed 18 Jul. 2025].

19 Szczys, M. (2021). *ASIC Miners, Mining Farm. 3D Rendering.* [online] Hackaday. Available at: https://hackaday.com/asic-miners-mining-farm-3d-rendering-4/ [Accessed 18 Jul. 2025].

20 Morey, M., McGrath, G. and Minato, H. (2024). *Tracking electricity consumption from U.S. cryptocurrency mining operations - U.S. Energy Information Administration (EIA).* [online] www.eia.gov. Available at: https://www.eia.gov/todayinenergy/detail.php?id=61364 [Accessed 21 Jul. 2025].

21 Hern, A. (2017). *Bitcoin mining consumes more electricity a year than Ireland.* [online] The Guardian. Available at:

https://www.theguardian.com/technology/2017/nov/27/bitcoin-mining-consumes-electricity-ireland [Accessed 21 Jul. 2025].

22 Song, J. (2019). *Programming Bitcoin.* United States of America: 'O'Reilly Media, Inc.', p.140.

23 Lacity, M.C. and Lupien, S.C. (2022). *Blockchain Fundamentals for Web 3.0.* University of Arkansas Press, p.54.

24 Burniske, C. and Tatar, J. (2018). *Cryptoassets : : The Innovative Investor's Guide to Bitcoin and Beyond /.* New York, N.Y.: Mcgraw-Hill Education, pp.110, 221-222, 339-340.

25 CoinMarketCap (2019). *All Cryptocurrencies | CoinMarketCap.* [online] CoinMarketCap. Available at: https://coinmarketcap.com/all/views/all/ [Accessed 25 Jul. 2025].

26 Antonopoulos, A.M. and Wood Ph.D, G. (2018). *Mastering Ethereum.* O'Reilly Media, pp. 43, 113-114, 304.

27 Sun, W., Wu, X. (Brian) and Kwok, A. (2019). *Security Tokens and Stablecoins Quick Start Guide : Learn How to Build STO and Stablecoin Decentralized Applications.* Birmingham: Packt Publishing, Limited, p.52.

28 Branson, E. (2014). *Ripple: The Ultimate Beginner's Guide for Understanding Ripple Currency And What You Need to Know (Beginner, Mining, Step by Step, Trading, Basics, XRP, Cryptocurrency)* . CreateSpace.

29 Debajani Mohanty (2019). *Ripple and Stablecoins : building banks of tomorrow : use cases on international remittance, capital and money markets, swaps, micropayments, trade finance, Islamic finance, and Stablecoins.* New Delhi: Manish Jain For Bpb Publications, pp.17–22, 31,33, 70-80.

30 Lacity, M.C. and Lupien, S.C. (2022). *Blockchain Fundamentals for Web 3.0.* University of Arkansas Press, p.140.

31 Debajani Mohanty (2019). *Ripple and Stablecoins : building banks of tomorrow : use cases on international remittance, capital and money markets, swaps, micropayments, trade finance, Islamic finance, and*

Stablecoins. New Delhi: Manish Jain For Bpb Publications, pp.90–95.

32 Tether (n.d.). *Transparency*. [online] tether.to. Available at: https://tether.to/en/transparency/?tab=usdt [Accessed 28 Jul. 2025].

33 CCI (2025). *What is an Algorithmic Stablecoin?* [online] Crypto Council for Innovation. Available at: https://cryptoforinnovation.org/what-is-an-algorithmic-stablecoin/ [Accessed 29 Jul. 2025].

34 Lacity, M.C. and Lupien, S.C. (2022). *Blockchain Fundamentals for Web 3.0*. University of Arkansas Press, p.142.

35 Unchained Crypto (2023). *What Are Ring Signatures? - Unchained Crypto*. [online] UnchainedCrypto. Available at: https://unchainedcrypto.com/ring-signatures/ [Accessed 30 Jul. 2025].

36 Burniske, C. and Tatar, J. (2018). *Cryptoassets : : The Innovative Investor's Guide to Bitcoin and Beyond /*. New York, N.Y.: Mcgraw-Hill Education, p.122.

37 CoinMarketCap (n.d.). *Top Privacy Tokens by Market Capitalization*. [online] CoinMarketCap. Available at: https://coinmarketcap.com/view/privacy/ [Accessed 30 Jul. 2025].

38 Pratap, J. (2023). *CBDC: What is CBDC and Which Countries Will Use Digital Currency?* [online] CoinGape. Available at: https://coingape.com/education/cbdc-what-is-cbdc-and-which-countries-will-use-digital-currency/ [Accessed 30 Jul. 2025].

39 Bank for International Settlements (2020). *Central bank digital currencies: foundational principles and core features*. [online] *bis.org*. Bank for International Settlements. Available at: https://www.bis.org/publ/othp33.pdf [Accessed 30 Jul. 2025].

40 Lacity, M.C. and Lupien, S.C. (2022). *Blockchain Fundamentals for Web 3.0*. University of Arkansas Press, p.138-139.

41 CoinMarketCap (2024). *Top Cryptocurrency Exchanges Ranked By Volume.* [online] CoinMarketCap. Available at: https://coinmarketcap.com/rankings/exchanges/ [Accessed 30 Jul. 2025].

7.Non Fungible Tokens

"The ability to create something which is not duplicable in the digital world has enormous value ... Lots of people will build businesses on top of that"
– Eric Schmidt

7.1 Introduction

The last chapter covered cryptocurrencies. Cryptocurrencies are just one type of token. They could be utility tokens as in the case of Ether, or serve as a means of exchange, like bitcoin does. In either case, cryptocurrencies are fungible. This means that one can exchange a given unit of a particular cryptocurrency with another equal unit of the same cryptocurrency without loss of value. Fiat currencies are also fungible. So a $100 bill can be exchanged with any other $100 bill with no change in value. This chapter introduces tokens which are non-fungible.

7.2 Tokens

A "token" is a blockchain-based abstraction that can be used to represent crypto currency, access rights or assets. It is derived from the word "tācen", which means a sign or symbol in Old English[1].

For centuries, proof of ownership of physical or financial assets has usually been provided in the form of paper documents like title deed, vehicle log book, share certificate, etc. When there is a change in ownership of an asset, the documents representing them must also be surrendered to the buyer or issuer, so that new documents can be prepared for the new owner. So in a sense these papers represent value. They are assets.

On blockchains, there are tokens that can be used to represent ownership of not just physical assets, but virtual assets as well. These tokens act like certificates of authenticity. Such tokens are referred to as security tokens. In the same manner that a document representing a specific physical asset is unique, security tokens are also unique[2]. They are non-fungible.

So we can define a Non Fungible Token (NFT) as "a form of digital asset whose ownership is recorded on a blockchain". The key benefits here are ease of transfer, immutability and provenance[3]. Once an individual has been recorded as an owner of an asset on a blockchain, it cannot be deleted. This makes it possible to see the history of ownership of the asset over time.

NFTs cannot be ignored. At the time of writing this section in August 2025, according to Forbes, the global NFT market cap was $131.48 Billion. A day prior to the date of access, the total trading volume for the day, was $7.82 Million[4].

7.3 Token Standards

Recall that cryptocurrencies or tokens in general, are essentially programs. So these programs are usually logically divided into named units that accomplish specific functions. Some program functions are applicable in many different products. For example, if it is a utility token or a means of exchange, there should be a function to check balance and another to transfer value. Other functions may also exist to suit the intention of the designers.

To enhance compatibility and interoperability with different wallets and market places, and also to make software code easier to audit, standards have been created to guide developers on how to write these programs. These standards are like templates or blueprints that can be used for development. Each blockchain might have its own standards.

For example, on the Ethereum network, fungible tokens are developed using the **ERC-20** standard. ERC stands for Ethereum Request for Comments. The number 20 that comes after ERC is just a unique ID number that distinguishes the fungible token standard from other standards.

The Ethereum community has also defined a general standard for NFTs (**ERC-721**) and other standards for unique assets such as identity claims (ERC-725) and collectibles (ERC-1155). ERC-721's primary purpose is to help track token ownership and any movements from a single, smart contract. Collectibles are among the most popular NFTs.

Whereas these standards were initially intended for the Ethereum blockchain, some of them have been implemented on other blockchains that support NFTs such as Tron, ICON, Ark, EOS and Steem[5].

There are very many other standards, which are beyond the scope of this book.

7.4 Origin of NFTs

The concept of NFTs first appeared around the period 2012 to 2013, on the Bitcoin blockchain. Here, "Colored Coins" were created to represent assets in the real world such as commodities like precious metals, or real estate or financial assets like equities and bonds. In essence "Colored Coins" are simply satoshis or bitcoins, repurposed for other uses besides money transfer. This was made possible through the insertion of unique metadata into the coin to specify what it could be used for, thus making the coin non-fungible[6].

However it was collectibles that gave NFTs their oomph. Collectibles include digital goods such computer images or real world physical art work that has been registered on a blockchain as one of a kind. This gives it rarity or scarcity and could raise the perceived monetary value of the item. One could argue that digital art work can just be copied, and that the copy is indistinguishable from the original. However, in the NFT world, if one cannot prove ownership of an item, then they cannot make money from it. That is why NFTs representing collectible art work were first called **monetized graphics** around the year 2014[7]. The obvious benefit here is that artists can get more money from their work directly, provided that they are the first to tokenize the said works. Buyers on the other hand get confidence that they are buying an original piece of work because its ownership history can be traced back to its creator on a blockchain.

It is mind boggling how much individuals are willing to pay for NFTs. For example, someone literally paid $ 2.9 million for the NFT of autographed, first tweet by Twitter co-founder Jack Dorsey[8]. Another person paid $ 500,000 for "Mars House", a virtual property designed by a Toronto artist by the name Krista Kim. In exchange for this amount of money, all that the buyer received were 3D files to upload to a Metaverse i.e. a virtual world[9]. Then there is the story of Chris Torres who sold an NFT of pixelated art of a cat that he had created years earlier for $ 690,000[10]. To view a list of the most expensive NFT sales of all time, you can visit nftnow.com[11].

7.5 Enterprise Use Cases for NFTs

NFTs can have many applications away from the creative industry such as music and art. However, most enterprise NFT applications are currently in their conceptual or experimental stages. This section will touch on a few use cases.

In academia, NFTs could be used to register trustworthy scientific papers thus making them immutable. Such a blockchain can then be used to verify references and aid in curbing plagiarism[12].

In the insurance industry, tokenization of policies can be used to automate payment of claims almost instantaneously. For example, if data is received into an insurance blockchain ecosystem associated with a certain policy, the system could automatically process payment and direct it to the policy holder (NFT owner). And what if a motor vehicle policy holder were to sell his car suddenly with 11 months remaining on the policy, could it be easier to sell this NFT to someone else, such that the new owner will enjoy all the benefits of the policy for the remaining period? [13]

In supply chain management, NFTs can be used to represent individual items. When an item(s) physically moves from the custody of one entity to another entity, ownership of the NFT representing it is also transferred to the new custodian's wallet. Location information can also be recorded automatically on the blockchain using scanners and be associated with the NFT. Eventually when the item lands at a store for sale, it is possible for conscious consumers to track its origin on the blockchain[14]. The types of items that can be tracked in this manner are unlimited.

NFTs can also be used for Identity and Access Management. As mentioned earlier, NFTs can be used to represent official documents. This includes identity documents like national IDs. So an NFT can be used to represent a person's digital Identity and be used to control access to some online services such as rated movies. Other than this, an organization could sell access tokens (NFTs) to individuals and use them to control access to physical facilities. In such cases, the token is being purchased for its utility value. To permit access, the organization's security system will check if the token is valid and if the person seeking entry owns it. The import of this is that, in some cases, access to some types of facilities could be sold on to other individuals. For example, if you purchased gym membership for a year and you receive a sudden promotion that necessitates a transfer to a faraway location, you could recover your money for the remaining period by selling your token to someone else. The gym shouldn't mind because they do not have to refund you money and then look for a replacement client[15]. Of course this last example would not apply in situations where membership is only granted after extensive background checks.

NFTs can enable fractional ownership of expensive assets such as real estate, aircrafts or yachts. For example, instead of selling a $500,000 aircraft to a single individual, 5 tokens can be minted and sold to 5 different people at $100,000 each. So the pool of buyers gets increased and liquidity is created for an asset that is traditionally non-bankable. The concept of fractional ownership permits buyers to own assets or enjoy services that they would otherwise not be able to afford. In most cases the allure to such assets is the possibility of value appreciation. So buying a fractional NFT can be considered as an investment and the NFT in question is a security. For this reason in some jurisdictions, fractional NFTs have to be registered with the relevant regulatory authorities like Securities and Exchange Commission (SEC) in the US[16].

7.6 NFTs from Creative Arts

In terms of market valuation, it is NFTs from rare prestige art that currently dominates. Art NFTs include collectibles, metaverse assets, trending memes and AI generated art.

Collectibles are simply any artworks that are deemed valuable and highly sought after. These could be images (photos), GIFs or digital trading cards.

Metaverse refers to virtual worlds on the internet like Decentraland and The Sandbox. In these worlds, assets like virtual land, buildings (e.g. virtual homes), avatars, wearables, names, vehicles, billboards are traded. The demand for metaverse assets is generated by the people who participate in virtual worlds.

Gaming NFTs follow a similar concept to those of the metaverse. For example a game would require characters (avatars), weapons if there are fights, skins etc. The creators of such assets can mint NFTs for them and trade them in market places. Pay attention to the fact that the games are developed to allow players to customize, for example, characters and clothe them as they please. So Gaming NFT assets are used for customization. Interestingly, in some cases, Gaming NFTs are compatible across many different games. This drives their value up.

NFTs can also be made for videos, 3D models, audios (music), books & prose. For example currently NFTs of video clips of iconic moments in NBA basketball are being made and sold at NBA TopShot, which is a specialized market place for such assets[17].

7.7 Creating Simple NFTs

From the previous sections, it can be seen that NFTs can be created for different things. There are many different tools that can be used to generate the mentioned assets. For example to create an image (picture) to be tokenized, you could use one, or a combination of popular desktop software like Adobe products or Corel draw. A quick search should reveal that plenty of free online tools are also available. Furthermore, with recent advances in Artificial Intelligence, one can literally type their ideas on a prompt and have a system generate something interesting that can be tokenized.

Once you have the asset you want to tokenize, two options are available for creating the NFT. The first one involves the use of a browser and NFT ecosystem sites like OpenSea, SuperRare or Rarible. You should have a wallet ready with some crypto because you might be required to pay for some of the services. The general procedure on such sites is to first open an account and associate a wallet with the account (done once).

The next step is to select the asset to be tokenized and then mint it. Minting is the term used to imply creating a token. This happens automatically without the user knowing the programmatic details for creating the token. Finally the token can be deployed on a blockchain such as Ethereum where it can be sold at a fixed price or be auctioned.

The second way, is to use software code i.e. write a smart contract using languages like Solidity. Once done, you can compile and get the contract deployed on your blockchain network. After that, you can mint the NFT using a function in the contract created for that purpose. Note that this method requires that you to specify in the code, among others, details like your account address and the path to your digital asset. In an NFT ecosystem site, the same details are input by filling-in forms and selecting options via lists and dialogue boxes. So the first method is easier and more common[18]. However the second method is more likely to be used when creating NFTs for enterprise applications.

7.8 Configuring NFTs

Irrespective of which route is chosen to mint an NFT, there are some important configurations that have to be done prior to creation. These help not just to enforce the creators' intentions, but to distinguish one NFT from another.

For example, the creator of an enterprise NFT might want to lease out tokens for a period of time. Here, reference is being made to tokens representing physical income generating assets, and from which the token creator wants to share revenue during the lease period. In other words, the buyers are lending the creator (business) money, for a period of time, and in return, earn a reasonable amount until the said period elapses, and then the creator returns the original amount to the buyers.

Another example is where an artist is selling an NFT but also intends to give a physical copy of the artwork to the buyer. The artist may also want to earn royalties perpetually i.e. a tiny percentage of any future sales of his or her NFT.

Configurations for enterprise NFTs are likely to done programmatically due to complexity, while those of collectibles can easily be specified on the forms provided by an NFT ecosystem site. Some common configurations, particularly for collectibles are as follows:

- Name: The full name should be provided. For example, currently we have NFTs with names such as Pudgy Penguins, CryptoPunks, Bored Ape Yatch Club etc

- Preview content: This is what a potential buyer of an NFT would see in a listing prior to taking an interest. It may include a catchy picture and a very brief description or slogan about the NFT.
- Main content: If the NFT is for an image or a video, then a link to it storage location may be specified. Note that for efficiency and prudent use of storage, most blockchains do not store media files on chain.
- Description: Any important information about the NFT that its creator would like the potential buyers to know.
- Traits: These are the NFT attributes that contribute to its rarity and value. For example if the NFT was based on cat images, color and size could be traits that distinguish one cat from another.
- Unlockable content: The purpose of unlockable content is to enhance the appeal of the NFT. Usually, the buyer will only be able access or benefit from the unlockable content after buying the NFT. It could be an additional physical gift that is sent to the buyer once the NFT has been paid for. For example if the NFT is created by a famous artist, the perk offered could be an autographed physical copy of another artwork.
- Ongoing royalty: The creator could elect to benefit from every subsequent resale of the NFT. For example if Tom buys it for $100 and later sells it to Mary for $150. Using a smart contract function, the creator could automatically be sent $5, assuming the royalty was set at 10% of all future profits. Later on, if Mary sells it on for $1500, the creator would receive $135.
- Supply: This serves to limit the total number of NFTs that can be minted for a given project. If an NFT is meant to be one of a kind, then the total supply should be

one. However, if the project is for a collection, then the NFTs would be more than one. In the latter case the number could be unlimited, fixed or dynamic. This decision should be made based of the nature of the NFT and the target market[19].

Note: In situations where an NFT seller is offering perks or unlockable content, contract law will come into play because the buyer might make the decision to buy an NFT strictly because of the perk, not the NFT itself. So if for example, an artist offered to have coffee with a buyer of an NFT as a perk, the seller must present himself/herself for the coffee date within the specified time period, or face legal action[20].

7.9 NFT Marketplaces

Whether you want to buy or sell an NFT, the place to do it is at an NFT marketplace. This is just like a cryptocurrency exchange, except that what is traded are NFTs.

Marketplaces provide services to generate, list and maintain NFTs in their systems (online galleries). So, depending on their individual business model, they may levy a form of registration (membership) fee, listing fee and also transaction fees after every sale[21].

There are many types of NFT marketplaces. Some require pre-approval before being allowed to list NFTs for sale, while others do not. Some are very specialized in that they list a very specific type of NFT only, while others are more generalized. Then there are those that allow payments using both cryptocurrencies and credit cards while others might permit only cryptocurrencies[22]. Finally there are exchanges which are centralized (Centralized Exchanges - CEX) and others which are decentralized (Decentralized Exchanges - DEX). It is usually on the CEXs like Bitfinex where the use of fiat currencies like USD is permitted. Fees charged on DEXs are generally lower than those of CEX, but only crypto is accepted[21].

Table 7.1 lists a few examples of NFT marketplaces, the blockchain they are based on, and a notable distinguishing factor.

Marketplaces	Blockchain	Differentiating factor
Opensea	Ethereum	for art, music, domain names, collectibles, and trading cards.
Nifty Gateway	Ethereum	only for established digital artists
SuperRare	Ethereum	only for single edition NFTs
NBA Top Shot	Flow	video NFTs of historical NBA moments
Rarible	Multichain i.e. Ethereum, Polygon, Solana, Tezos , and Flow	allows users to mint NFTs on various supported networks
Theta Drop	Theta Network	offer decentralized video and TV distribution on the internet.

Table 7.1 Examples of NFT Marketplaces

For a creator, a key determining factor on which marketplace to list an NFT on, is the blockchain on which it was minted. Ordinarily, a marketplace will support an NFT that has been minted on the same network as itself. For example an NFT minted on Ethereum should be compatible with any marketplace that is also based on Ethereum. However, there are marketplaces like Rarible that allow the listing of NFTs from several different blockchain networks.

At the moment, most NFTs are based on the Ethereum blockchain. However, many other blockchain networks are maturing in that respect. These include Tron, Flow, Polkadot, WAX, Cosmos, EOS, Tezos, and Binance Smart Chain. As expected, each of these has its own NFT token standards, compatible wallet services, and marketplaces[22].

7.10 Concerns against NFTs

There are some NFT projects that are constantly evolving in order to give the community new experiences or features. Examples include metaverse, gaming and art collection projects. It must not be assumed that they will continue perpetually because a project could run out of money, or face some other challenge that could suddenly bring it to a halt[23].

Secondly, in the case of creative art, there are intellectual property rights concerns. Some marketplaces have no way of verifying whether the individuals minting NFTs are the original creators of the work. Granted, there are some marketplaces that restrict the listing of artwork for sale or auction to established (known) artists. Nevertheless, the potential for fraudsters to benefit off the work of others, who might not even be aware of NFTs, still exists. To make matters worse, whereas the crypto transactions used to trade NFTs are transparent, the participants are not easily identified. This makes it easier for fraudulent activities to occur[24].

Thirdly, an NFT owner's wallet could be hacked, leading to the theft of his NFTs[23].

The fourth concern mainly affects enterprise NFTs. Unlike those for creative arts, these ones require a high level of customization, and so form templates would not work. The NFTs must be created programmatically. However, getting knowledgeable, experienced, affordable and available smart contract developers might not be easy. This is likely to change with time.

The fifth concern is the speculative nature of some NFT investments. Consider Sina Estavi who bought an NFT of a tweet for $2.9m. Later when he attempted to auction it for $48m, the highest bid he got was only $6,800[8]. Some NFTs have no inherent value and people just buy them as a result of irrational speculation. Others have meaning or sentimental value only to the buyer, at a particular time, when the buyer is willing to spend well above the true value. Later on, when the new owner wants to sell it, he realizes no one else values the product that much. A lot of patience and luck may help in recouping the money spent, but this is highly unlikely.

Lastly, as regulators swoop in to the NFT space, investors should expect time consuming red tape bureaucracy and heavy taxation. Some of the speed, efficiency, anonymity and decentralization hitherto touted as benefits of blockchains may be lost as some central control is reintroduced by government. Already with NFTs categorized as securities in some jurisdictions, investors are expected to pay sales taxes and capital gains taxes[23].

Conclusion

NFTs are digital representations of both digital and physical assets that are registered on a blockchain. In a sense they act as official paper documents. Leveraging on the benefits of blockchain technology such as provenance and immutability, it is possible to determine the origin of the asset, authenticity of ownership and the uniqueness of the asset. Being tokens like cryptos, NFTs are easier and faster to transact with, in comparison to traditional property transfer methods.

For artists, NFTs allow them to interact directly with buyers of their work instead of relying on middlemen. NFTs are essentially smart contracts, so they make it possible for artists to be paid royalties automatically and directly. Suffice it to say that in comparison to traditional art market model, NFTs enable artists to earn a better living from their work.

From an investment perspective, fractional NFTs create a new asset class and can inject liquidity into hitherto cash strapped industries.

However, the entry of regulators into the NFT/Crypto space may be a boon in terms of reducing fraudulent activities, but at the same time, it might stifle and discourage innovation.

Exercise 7

1. Briefly outline the differences among utility tokens, means of exchange and security tokens.

2. Briefly describe STO (Security Token Offering).

3. List five differences between an ICO and an STO.

i. ______________________

____

____

ii. ______________________

____

____

iii. ______________________

____

____

iv. ______________________

____

____

v. ______________________

Quiz 7

1 Complete the following statement.
All of the following are fungible except ________________.

a) tokenized physical assets
b) fiat currency
c) US dollar
d) Bitcoin

2 Which of the following statements is **false**?

a) A blockchain is only required for the transfer and storage of NFT information.
b) Token standards are the same across all blockchains.
c) An NFT is a form of digital asset whose ownership is recorded on a blockchain.
d) Tokens that are used to represent ownership, act like certificates of authenticity.

3 Which of the following statements about security tokens are **true**? (you may choose one or more)

i. Unlike fungible tokens, security tokens are not recorded on a blockchain.
ii. Security tokens can be used for access management.
iii. Security tokens are synonymous with certificates of ownership and authenticity.
iv. Security tokens can be used to represent physical or digital assets.

a) i only
b) i and iii
c) ii, iii and iv
d) All of the above

4 Complete the following statement.
On the Ethereum network, the general standard for NFTs is ________________________.

a) ERC-20
b) ERC-1155
c) ERC-721

d) ERC-725

5 Which of the following statements is **true**?

a) NFTs cannot be used to represent official documents like national IDs.

b) In terms of market valuation, it is enterprise NFTs that currently dominates, compared to NFTs from rare prestige art.

c) NFTs can be used to facilitate fractional ownership of expensive assets such as real estate, aircrafts or yachts.

d) Creating NFTs to represent trustworthy scientific papers cannot help in reducing plagiarism.

6 Complete the following statement.

Art NFTs includes ________________________________.

a) videos, 3D models, audios (music), books & prose

b) virtual worlds on the internet like Decentraland and The Sandbox

c) enterprise NFTs

d) collectibles, metaverse assets, trending memes and AI generated art

7 Which of the following **best** describes NFT marketplaces ?

a) They are online ecosystems where one can mint an NFT.

b) They are like online galleries where one can buy or sell an NFT.

c) They are just like cryptocurrency exchanges.

d) They can be centralized but are mostly decentralized.

8 Which of the following statements regarding STOs are **false**? (you may choose one or more)

i. STO processes involve intermediaries such as lawyers.

ii. A STO issues a security token, which is a digital stock certificate.

iii. STOs are limited by geographic borders and are not open to more investors over the internet.

iv. The security token issuer can interact directly with investors on the designated STO offering platform.

a) iii only
b) i and iii
c) i, ii and iv
d) ii, iii and iv

9 Which of the following is **not** a configuration item for art NFTs?

a) Buyer's name
b) Supply
c) Ongoing royalty
d) Unlockable content

10 Which of the following statements are concerns regarding NFTs? (you may choose one or more)

i. Intellectual property rights violations when individuals create NFT of other people's work and benefit financially from the same.
ii. NFT projects will continue perpetually.
iii. Regulation will bring about efficiency and considerate taxation.
iv. An NFT owner's wallet could be hacked, leading to the theft of his NFTs.

a) i only
b) ii and iii
c) iii and iv
d) i and iv

References

1 Antonopoulos, A.M. and Wood Ph.D, G. (2018). *Mastering Ethereum.* O'Reilly Media, p.424.

2 Sun, W., Wu, X. (Brian) and Kwok, A. (2019). *Security Tokens and Stablecoins Quick Start Guide : Learn How to Build STO and Stablecoin Decentralized Applications.* Birmingham: Packt Publishing, Limited, p.113.

3 Ellis, W. (2021). *Non-Fungible Tokens explained : simplest practical guide to everything you need to know about NFTs (the crypto art selling) including creating an NFT from start to finish.* Great Britain: S.N, pp.5–6, 14.

4 Forbes (2025). *NFT Collection Prices & Charts Today By Trading Volume.* [online] Forbes.com. Available at: https://www.forbes.com/digital-assets/nft-prices/?sh=68070cb26dfb [Accessed 20 Aug. 2025].

5 Marswood, Matt.J. (2021). *NFT For Beginners: Guide To The World of Non-Fungible Tokens and Cryptoart.* Matt J. Marswood, pp.10, 8.

6 Trust Machines (2015). *What Are Colored Coins and How Do They Relate to Bitcoin?* [online] Trustmachines.co. Available at: https://trustmachines.co/learn/what-are-colored-coins/ [Accessed 20 Aug. 2025].

7 Fortnow, M. and Terry, Q. (2021). *NFT HANDBOOK : how to create, sell and buy non -fungible tokens.* S.L.: John Wiley, p.109.

8 Reuters (2022). *Man who paid $2.9m for NFT of Jack Dorsey's first tweet set to lose almost $2.9m.* [online] the Guardian. Available at: https://www.theguardian.com/technology/2022/apr/14/twitter-nft-jack-dorsey-sina-estavi [Accessed 21 Aug. 2025].

9 Kolirin, L. (2021). *World's first digital NFT house sells for $500,000.* [online] CNN. Available at: https://edition.cnn.com/style/article/digital-nft-mars-house-scli-intl [Accessed 21 Aug. 2025].

10 Maidan, L. (2022). *How a cat GIF NFT sold for about $690,000:*

Creator explains process. [online] Business Insider. Available at: https://www.businessinsider.com/nyan-cat-nft-sold-creator-explains-gif-process-2022-1?r=US&IR=T [Accessed 21 Aug. 2025].

11 Thomas, L. (2022). *The 15 Most Expensive NFT Sales of All Time.* [online] nft now. Available at: https://nftnow.com/features/most-expensive-nft-sales/ [Accessed 21 Aug. 2025].

12 Emurgo (2024). *5 Practical NFT Real-World Use Cases* . [online] Emurgo.io. Available at: https://www.emurgo.io/press-news/5-practical-nft-real-world-use-cases/ [Accessed 22 Aug. 2025].

13 Lewis, M. (2022). *10 Ways Enterprise NFTs Will Change How We Do Business.* [online] Kaleido.io. Available at: https://www.kaleido.io/blockchain-blog/enterprise-nft-examples [Accessed 22 Aug. 2025].

14 Hedera (2021). *NFT Use Cases: Creative Ideas for a Revolutionary Tool | Hedera.* [online] Hedera. Available at: https://hedera.com/learning/nfts/nft-use-cases [Accessed 22 Aug. 2025].

15 IMI (2023). *NFT Adoption in Identity and Access Management - Identity Management Institute®.* [online] Identity Management Institute®. Available at: https://identitymanagementinstitute.org/nft-adoption-in-identity-and-access-management/ [Accessed 22 Aug. 2025].

16 Fortnow, M. and Terry, Q. (2021). *NFT HANDBOOK : how to create, sell and buy non -fungible tokens.* S.L.: John Wiley, pp.247-250.

17 Shahbazi, N. (2025). *Breakthrough 10 Major Types of NFTs + Example (2025).* [online] Pixune. Available at: https://pixune.com/blog/different-types-of-nfts/ [Accessed 22 Aug. 2025].

18 Souza, J. (2023). *How to create an NFT with your own image art.* [online] Medium. Available at:

https://medium.com/@juliano641/how-to-create-an-nft-with-your-own-image-art-6752c4fb9134 [Accessed 21 Aug. 2025].

19 nft-inator (2023). *Optimizing Your NFT Collection Supply for Success.* [online] nft-inator.com. Available at: https://nft-inator.com/blog/optimizing-your-nft-collection-supply [Accessed 22 Aug. 2025].

20 Fortnow, M. and Terry, Q. (2021). *NFT HANDBOOK : how to create, sell and buy non -fungible tokens.* S.L.: John Wiley, pp.232-233, 235-237.

21 Marswood, Matt.J. (2021). *NFT For Beginners: Guide To The World of Non-Fungible Tokens and Cryptoart.* Matt J. Marswood, pp.71-78, 80-81.

22 Ellis, W. (2021). *Non-Fungible Tokens explained : simplest practical guide to everything you need to know about NFTs (the crypto art selling) including creating an NFT from start to finish.* Great Britain: S.N, pp.9, 27, 32, 21-22.

23 Fortnow, M. and Terry, Q. (2021). *NFT HANDBOOK : how to create, sell and buy non -fungible tokens.* S.L.: John Wiley, pp.208, 234, 235, 237

24 Ellis, W. (2021). *Non-Fungible Tokens explained : simplest practical guide to everything you need to know about NFTs (the crypto art selling) including creating an NFT from start to finish.* Great Britain: S.N, p.12.

8. Self-Sovereign Identity

"The person I was waiting for was me. I could authorize my own choice. I could choose my own validation with sovereignty."
- Madison Morrigan

8.1 Introduction

The original idea behind the internet was the inter-connection of geographically dispersed computers in order to facilitate the sharing of information and other resources.

Whereas this was successful, the design did not adequately address the problem of user authentication. As a result, the growth of the internet has been accompanied by rising cases of hacking. Hacking is characterized by unauthorized access to, or interference with a system, in order to disrupt service provision, alter data, or steal data. This problem's significance is such that a former IBM President and CEO, Ginni Rometty, once described cybercrime as "the greatest threat to every profession, every industry, every company in the world"[1].

One method that has been employed to curb cybercrime is to manage access by first identifying users and then depending on the service(s) being offered, different levels of access may be granted. This has not always been very effective. So, as the internet has evolved with time, so have identity models.

8.2 Internet Identity Models

Since the initial form of the internet, to establish an identity, an individual has had to register an account with each service provider. Typically this involves creating a username and password on each website of interest. This is referred to as

account-based identity and it follows a **centralized identity model**[2].

Later on, some organizations started providing the option for users to access multiple sites through a single account managed by them. This is called the **federated identity** model and is facilitated by organizations like Facebook, Google, Amazon and LinkedIn.

The problem with centralized and federated identity models is that, users' data is controlled and monetized by institutions, with disregard to its owners.

A third identity model is **Self-Sovereign Identity (SSI)**, which is decentralized. Its objective is to shift control over identities and credentials, from corporates to their owners, hence the term 'self-sovereign'[3]. Since SSI identity model is based on peer-to-peer relationships between any two entities, it includes client-server relationships as well. This makes it a broader model compared to centralized ones[4].

In the same manner in which we carry credentials like national ID cards or insurance cards in our physical wallets, SSI technology enables the creation of digital SSI wallets in which, we can carry digital versions of our credentials. Actually, SSI technology goes a step further and provides mechanisms by which these credentials can be granted by authorized issuers and delivered directly into an entity's SSI wallet. Since the credentials are digital in nature, it is possible to receive into the SSI wallet, credentials that would otherwise not fit into a physical wallet like a University degree[5].

8.3 SSI Definition

SSI is a model for digital identity on the internet that is not under the control any other authority[6]. It defines standards that guide how personal data control and identity management should work across digital networks[7], thus automating authenticity, integrity and validity checks, without being locked into platforms that are proprietary[8]. In effect, this facilitates decentralized issuance, storage, verification and renewal of credentials[5].

Moreover with SSI, individuals have the choice of selective disclosure of personal information, and can limit it to a need to know basis. So even administrative systems in SSI ecosystems would not request, receive or store more personal information than is necessary in order to comply with data privacy laws.

SSI is actually a set of technologies that encompasses Identity Management, distributed ledger technology (Blockchain), cryptography, and distributed computing. A key contribution to SSI from Blockchain technology is the new alternative for implementing a decentralized public key infrastructure (DPKI) system[9].

Note: Public Key Infrastructure (PKI) is a framework for secure communications. It manages public-private key pairs as well as digital certificates in order to facilitate authentication of users, devices, and services. PKI is centralized in its operation.

8.4 Building Blocks of SSI

SSI has seven building blocks, which are as follows: (1) Verifiable credentials or digital credentials (2) The trust triangle (3) Digital wallets (4) Digital agents (5) Decentralized Identifiers (DIDs) (6) Blockchains and other verifiable data registries (7) Governance frameworks or trust frameworks[7].

(1) Verifiable credentials (VCs)

Chadwick and Burnett (2021) referred to Verifiable Credentials as "the hero of the SSI show"[10]. A credential implies a cryptographically secured, digital version of both paper and digital proofs about yourself, like your national identity or a qualification like a diploma certificate[11]. They can be issued and digitally verified automatically, upon request, in a secure and trustworthy way within seconds or even milliseconds.

Besides individuals, VCs can also be issued to non-humans entities like companies, authorities and machines. An example of a machine that can be issued with a VC is an IoT (Internet of Things) sensor device in a manufacturing setting[12].

A VC consists of four parts which are collectively referred to as a VC package. See **Figure 8.1.** The first part contains a unique identifier for the credential. The second part contains the claims made by the credential e.g. if the credential is an ID of sorts, it might have the name, date of birth, sex, hair color, eye color, height etc.

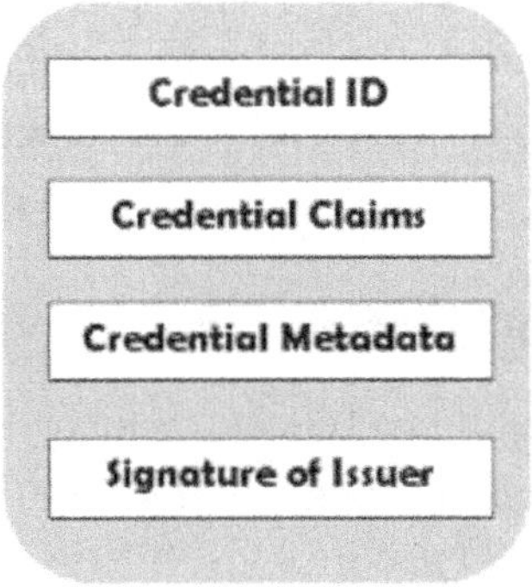

Figure 8.1: Structure of a Verifiable Credential[13]

The next part contains data about the credential itself, such as the date of issue for a student ID. Finally we have the cryptographically generated digital signature of the entity who issued the credential.

The use of cryptography makes VCs tamper evident and thus more trustworthy in comparison to physical credentials. In addition, since they are designed to be transmitted and verified with speed, they are convenient, and enable trust even at a distance, including across national or even continental boundaries[14].

(2) Trust Triangle

This depicts the interaction among issuers, holders, and verifiers. See **figure 8.2.**

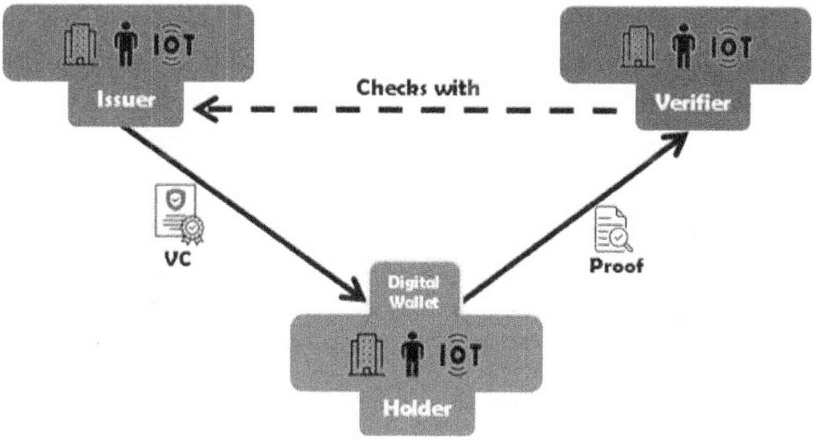

Figure 8.2: Relationship between issuers, holders and verifiers in an SSI ecosystem[13]

Credentials come from Issuers. Whereas most issuers are likely to be institutions, individuals and machines can also assume this role. For example, an SSI enabled camera could issue a digitally signed credential about a photo taken at a particular time.

Holders could be individuals, or organizations, or things that request for VCs from issuers, and then hold them in their digital wallet. Upon request by verifiers, and by agreement of the holder, the holder can present proofs of claims from one or more credentials to the verifier. Holders are also referred to as provers.

Verifiers seek a trust assurance of some kind about the subjects of credentials. Like issuers and holders, verifiers can be a person, an organization, or a thing. Subject to a holder's agreement, the holder's agent responds with a proof that the verifier can then verify. Note that the verifier does not have to have a direct business or legal relationship with the issuer, in the same way an employer does not have to have a relationship with a university. The employer (verifier) simply needs to recognize the university's legal existence and competence (issuer) and be able to verify that they have in fact issued a certain qualification (VC) to a certain individual (holder)[13].

(3) Digital wallets

If one is familiar with mobile wallets and cryptocurrency wallets, then an SSI wallet is similar, but it has two major additional distinguishing features. The first one is that implementation of open standards to support portability of self-sovereign VCs as well as other sensitive private data, is a mandatory requirement for an SSI digital wallet. Secondly, an SSI wallet has a digital agent that forms connections and performs credential exchanges on behalf of the holder.

These requirements are necessary so as to enable SSI wallets to function like general-purpose digital wallets rather than proprietary wallets from different vendors, where each wallet uses that vendor's own APIs and VC designs. The whole idea is to have SSI wallets mimic real-world, physical wallets that we carry in our pockets. Put differently, an SSI wallet should be able to accept any VC, if its design is based on certain standards. Secondly, an SSI wallet can be hosted on any device. Thirdly contents of an SSI wallet can be backed up or transferred to other digital wallets irrespective of vendors, if necessary. Lastly, a user's experience should be the same across devices made by different vendors.

A key feature of SSI wallets is that they automatically maintain an encrypted backup of your digital wallet. Consequently, compared to physical wallets, they are more secure from loss, theft, or hacking[15].

Currently there are two types of SSI wallets i.e. "Edge wallets" and "cloud wallets".

With edge wallets, the wallet itself, resides on the person's device. It is considered a more "pure" solution because individuals do not rely on a third-party provider. They have complete ownership, control, and management of their own wallet and keys. Most SSI wallets are edge wallets.

Unlike for edge wallets where processing is done on the device itself, cloud wallets have theirs done on a server in the cloud, thus making their implementation comparatively lightweight. It is also flexible, since the same wallet can be viewed via mobile app or through a browser, which is not possible for edge wallets. Ideally, a cloud wallet owner should be able to export their wallet out of the cloud and into an edge wallet, if they so desire. Without this capability, we would not really have self-sovereignty. The main disadvantage of Cloud wallets is that they require that the user have internet connectivity[16].

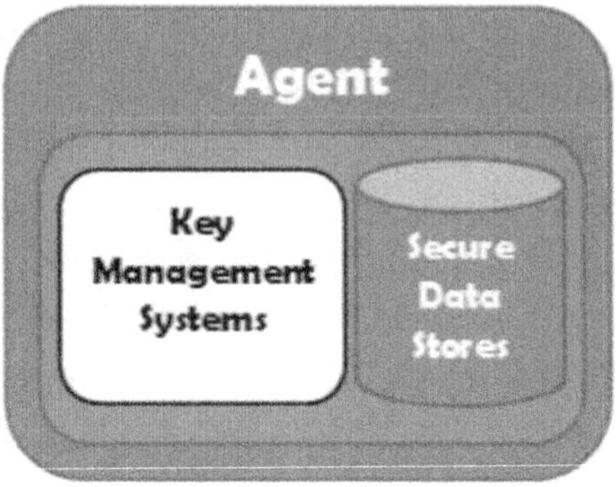

Figure 8.3: Digital wallet[17]

(4) Digital agents

Also known as Identity agents, digital agents are software modules in the SSI infrastructure that operates wallets on behalf of their owner. They protect digital wallets to ensure that only the owner of VCs and wallet cryptographic keys can use them. See **Figure 8.3**.

Under the directive(s) of their owners, digital agents can connect to exchange credentials with each other over the internet, through a decentralized, secure messaging protocol designed for private communication between digital agents. Other tasks carried out by digital agents include back up and retrieval of data in the wallet, management of encrypted data interactions, signing of outgoing documents and verification of signatures in incoming documents.

Agents are generally categorized into two, in reflection of the two types of wallets i.e. Edge and cloud wallets. Edge agents operate on an identity holder's local devices. They are said to operate on the "edge of the network".

Cloud agents, as hosts of standard cloud computing platform providers, or specialized cloud service providers (**agencies**), operate in the cloud. Some of them can be used to synchronize with edge devices, content such as files and/or photos on behalf of an identity owner. The different wallet apps used for access are thus required to be compatible with different SSI agencies.

An important feature of cloud storage in SSI infrastructure that differs from traditional cloud storage is that, identity holder encrypt their own data, just like is possible on edge devices. To reflect on this benefit, the term **secure data stores** (SDS) is used. Some literature differentiates between such data stores and label them differently, based on actual content and level of security. So you could also come across terms like **vault** or **personal data store** (PDS).

Conceptually a single digital agent is often paired with a single wallet. However, an implementation may have it such that a single digital agent manages multiple separate wallets. Conversely, and especially in an enterprise scenario, multiple agents could be designed have access to a single wallet[18].

(5) Decentralized identifiers (DIDs)

DIDs are globally unique, cryptographic identifiers that function as Uniform Resource Identifiers (URIs). Unlike other identifiers that are created to be used within an existing context (environment), DIDs are first created then contextualized i.e. shared to be used for specific connections.

The creator of a DID maintains complete authority over it, without the risk of revocation by any central authority, thus increasing censorship resistance. The decentralized nature of DIDs makes it scalable and conducive for a worldwide SSI infrastructure, in which each individual participant is managing a number of pairs of cryptographic keys. Moreover, unlike PKI, it does not portend a single point of failure.

Any two DIDs can be used to establish a secure connection using the SSI protocol stack, in a similar manner in which two IP addresses can form a connection using the TCP/IP protocol stack. However, unlike IP addresses and other identifiers like domain names, email addresses or mobile numbers, DIDs cannot be reassigned, which makes them a more secure and private mechanism.

Currently two types of DIDs exist. The first, Peer DIDs, is used for private, pairwise relationships, and can therefore be exchanged directly between the participants. The other, Public DIDs are used for arbitrary resolution of DIDs by anyone. Therefore, they must be recorded on a public DID repository such as blockchains.

Nevertheless, a DID usually resolves to a DID document that contains access points of at least one public key and one service, besides other metadata. Once entities have obtained and resolved each other's DIDs, they can use cryptographic keys for mutually authentication in order to communicate securely[19]. Figure 8.4 depicts a DID connection between two wallets.

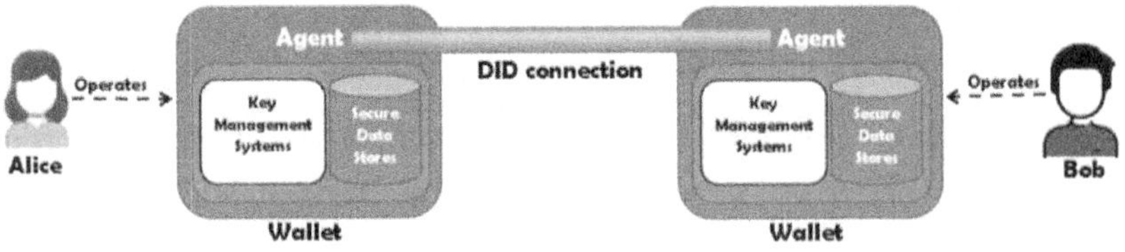

Figure 8.4: DID connection between two wallets[15]

(6) Blockchains and other verifiable data registries:

From the previous section, a DID can be exchanged peer-to-peer, or registered with any type of decentralized network. When a DID is registered on a blockchain, the formal term used is **verifiable data registry** (VDR). See **Figure 8.5.** The rationale for using blockchain as verifiable data registry is that blockchain is a decentralized, immutable transactional database that is not under the control of a single party. Blockchain can therefore serve as an authoritative source of data that is trusted by many different peers.

In an SSI ecosystem, blockchains are used to register DIDs and public keys. Communicating parties can then use such a VDR to resolve a DID to a public key, which then enables digital wallets and digital agents to securely communicate and exchange VCs. VDRs provide the strong foundation required for the universal adoption of the verifiable digital credentials, which is at the heart of SSI[20].

Figure 8.5 depicts the interaction between Issuers and Verifiers with a Verifiable Data Registry.

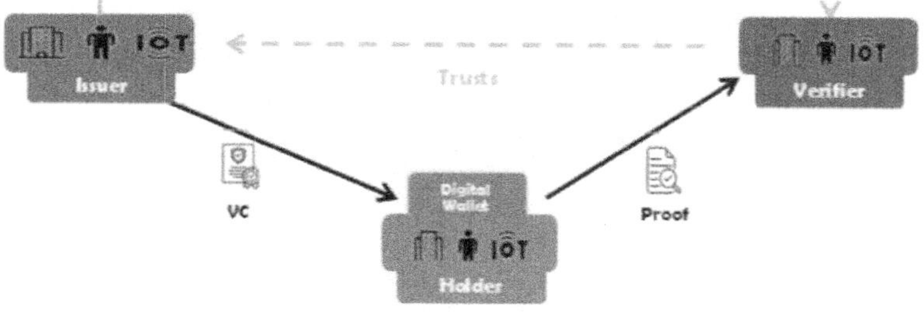

Figure 8.5: Verifiable Data Registry[21, 13]

(7) Governance frameworks

These are a set rules created and administered by an entity known as the governance authority. They are also known as Trust Framework, because they serve to facilitate a level of trust that is mutually agreeable for any two communicating entities on the internet.

Governance frameworks can be designed to meet technical, business, and legal requirements. For example, they can be used to provide guidance to issuers on the policies and/or procedures that must be followed to issue a credential. They may also specify the terms and conditions to which a participant such as a verifier or holder must agree to, to carry out their role. Finally, a governance authority can specify in their frameworks, business models to be used for credential exchange.

Figure 8.6 depicts how a governance framework can make a verifier's task easier.

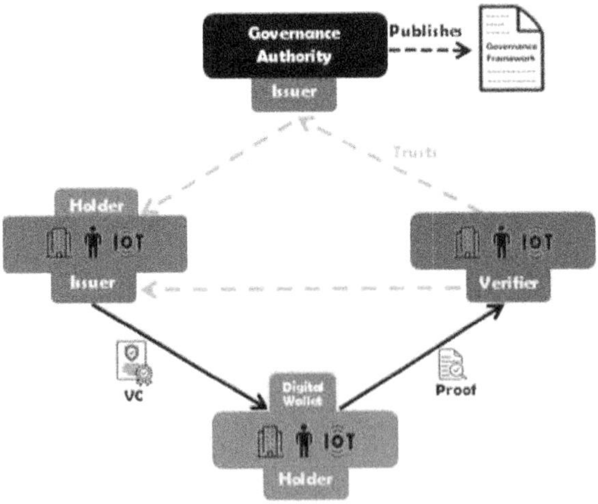

Figure 8.6: Complete trust triangle[22]

Notice how a governance framework creates the second trust triangle shown in the upper half of the figure.

Any time a holder presents proof to a verifier from an issuer that is unknown to the verifier, the verifier checks if the issuer is adhering to a governance framework that the verifier trusts. The check could entail searching a common repository such as a secure directory or scanning a simple "whitelist" or a blockchain. It may also involve verifying that the issuer has a valid VC from a known governance authority

The design of trust triangles involving governance frameworks as depicted in figure 8.6, can work for any size of trust community including global ones, even in situations where verifiers have no direct relations with, or any knowledge of all the issuers[22].

8.5 Some Potential Benefits/Features of SSI

SSI is still a budding technology. However it is already evident from its features that SSI has the potential to improve business efficiencies, user experiences and regulatory oversight. Some of these features are covered below:

1) Auto Authentication

Passwords are currently still being used to control access to many services. However the general attitude towards them is negative. They can be cumbersome to use, complex to remember, easy to steal and if they protect valuable resources, a lost or leaked password can be expensive.

Using DID based password-less authentication, SSI provides a more secure and convenient method for identity verification, completely eliminating traditional concerns. In this system, users (i.e. their digital agent) present their DID and some cryptographic proof that they have control over the presented DID. No password is necessary[23].

2) Auto Authorization

Authorization refers to the privileges granted based on the information that the customer has provided. The level of authorization is typically determined when signing up for a service by filling forms. Most users are turned off by the requirement to fill forms, particularly if they are lengthy.

Just like for authentication, the user's SSI agent can provide only the required information and in some cases only provide proof of meeting requirements without disclosing the information from which the proof is derived. For example, if the service requires the user to be over 18yrs, then the SSI agent will not present the date of birth. Instead it provides cryptographic proof that the user is over 18. This is known as Zero Knowledge Proof (ZKP).

Therefore with SSI authorization can be automated in such a manner that respective agents exchange all necessary information while creating an audit trail for accountability, thereby bringing about efficiency and better user experience by removing the need to fill forms[24].

3) Workflow Automation

Auto authentication and authorization are actually a form of workflow automation. But this can be extended further by programming digital agents with business logic, so that they can carry out some tasks automatically.

Depending on the business scenario, digital agents can either be pre-programmed to run certain scripts or they could be programmed to dynamically determine what SSI connections are necessary for a task and then download and run scripts from those connections, in order to accomplish certain business objectives.

With SSI it is possible to achieve a worldwide Business Process Automation (BPA) because "SSI enables BPA workflows to be carried out across any set of trust boundaries, according to any set of policies agreed to by the participants"[25].

From a user perspective, workflow automation can reduce both the time and effort required to accomplish certain tasks. For example, traditionally, if a user needs to update certain information about themselves with certain entities, the user has to edit forms on each entity's platform after going through separate authentication processes. With SSI, the user can simply update the information in the store where their agent usually accesses it, and then instructs their SSI agent to locate all entities that have the old information and update them. Ordinarily, such a task could easily take tens of minutes, if not hours, yet with SSI, it could be reduced to just a minute or two[26].

4) Data Security, Privacy & Protection

Cybercriminals often target access credentials of many people under the control of one organization such as a bank or crypto exchange. With SSI, this is not possible because user agents often establish private, secure channels for each communication partner. In each case, a different private-public key pair may be in use and the private keys are all stored locally in an encrypted form. Therefore to impersonate someone, an attacker must try to steal private keys one at a time. This is a formidable task even for a single target. In most cases, the price will not be worth the effort.

For data to remain accurate, it must be kept up to date. In some cases, the company holding a user's data is no longer authorized to keep it. As mentioned earlier, SSI user agents can make update requests. In addition, they can also make a digitally signed request for erasure of data and later verify if the request was honored.

Using SSI it is easier for organizations to comply with government regulations regarding data using features like selective disclosure, ZKP and verifiable consent. Verifiable consent allows an individual to be able to trace through their SSI agent whether a company obtained direct permission to hold his or her data, and if not, where they got it from. Furthermore, SSI governance frameworks that represent the interests of all stake holders can replace company specific policies and be implemented in such a manner that user agents can automatically verify regulatory approval before compliance. Under this kind of setup, movement of data between systems would be in conformity to security, privacy, and control requirements of data protection regulations[27].

5) Guardianship & Delegation credentials

The designers of SSI have considered that there are some individuals who might not be in a position to operate SSI technology independently, either due to age or the lack of a personal SSI enabled device. So they made it possible to give instructions and assign responsibilities to digital agents via program code using a subclass of verifiable credentials called **guardianship credentials**.

Using guardianship credentials, an entity can operate SSI agents and wallets on behalf of another entity. The entity bestowed with this responsibility is called a **digital guardian**. Digital guardianship is a form of "complete delegation" and equates to a guardianship order from a court. This is a great way to extend the benefits of SSI so that they can be enjoyed by any person irrespective of their capacity, be it mental, physical, or financial.

There is yet another subclass of verifiable credentials called **delegation credentials**. It can be used by an entity to grant partial responsibility to another entity. For example, using it the Department of Civil Registration could grant some hospitals the authority to register new births on behalf of parents[28].

8.6 SSI in Action

Let's assume an environment where the presiding government not only officially recognizes VCs, but participates and acts as a governance authority. Using delegation credentials, it grants some hospitals the authority to register new births with the Department of Civil Registration on behalf of parents.

So let's assume Alice gives birth to a son who she names John. When being discharged from the hospital, using her government issued SSI credential,

1. Alice makes a request to the hospital for a birth certificate via her phone, probably initiating the transaction by scanning the hospital's QR code in the maternity wing.
2. The hospital's enterprise wallet's agent connects with Alice's wallet agent and requests for the necessary details for birth registration.
3. Alice's wallet agent provides these details e.g. John's name and John's father's name etc.
4. The hospital's agent connects to the Department of Civil Registrations, to share this birth registration details.
5. Alice is requested to accept a direct connection to Department of Civil Registrations.
6. Alice accepts

7. The connection to the hospital agent is closed while one to Department of Civil Registrations is opened.
8. As part of "Get birth certificate" workflow, Department of Civil Registrations recommends a wallet app (John's wallet) to Alice, which she agrees to install.
9. Department of Civil Registrations issues Alice with a signed digital birth certificate (VC) for John, recognized by the government and trusted by any entity that trusts the government.
10. Department of Civil Registrations issues Alice with a signed guardianship credential for John, permitting, Alice to fully operate John's wallet as her own.
11. The Department of Civil Registrations terminates connection to Alice and requests a connection to John's wallet.
12. Alice accepts and the connection to Alice's wallet is terminated
13. The Department of Civil Registrations establishes a connection to John's wallet.
14. Department of Civil Registrations issues John with a signed digital birth certificate (VC).
15. Finally, the connection to John's wallet is terminated.

Note: All this takes place in less than a minute or two. Figure 8.7 summarizes these interactions.

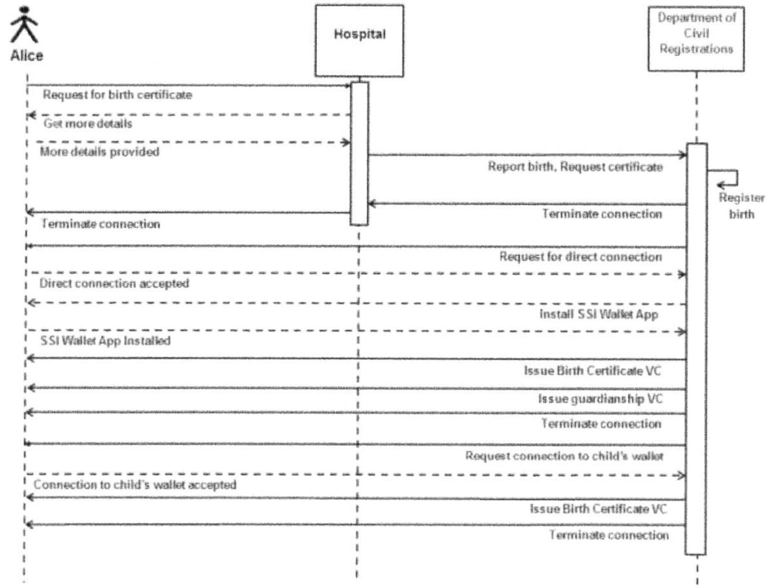

Figure 8.7: A sequence diagram depicting the general interactions between Alice, the hospital and the Department of Civil Registrations[29].

The above steps are just an outline which could be improved upon and made to work in real life.

Conclusion

SSI is an identity model that gives back control of user data to its owner, while at the same time bringing convenience to the user.

Businesses that employ SSI are likely to gain financially from improved e-commerce sales, reduction in fraud, time savings for its personnel and reduced customer service costs. SSI also makes it easier for business to comply with data security and privacy related regulations.

Finally, for regulators, SSI governance framework makes it easier to specify policies, update policies, and to audit for compliance in real time and at a much cheaper cost.

The future of self-sovereign identity is indeed very exciting.

Exercise 8

1. Briefly Compare and contrast SSI DIDs with Domain Name Service (DNS) names.

____

____

____

____

____

____

____

____

2. Briefly describe a scenario depicting how SSI based Regulation Technology (RegTech) would work.

____

____

____

____

____

____

3. List any five Blockchains that are purpose-built for SSI.

i. ______________________________

ii. ______________________________

iii. ______________________________

iv. ______________________________

v. ______________________________

Quiz 8

1 Three of the following are internet identity models. Which one is not?

a) Centralized Identity
b) Self-Sovereign Identity
c) Federated Identity
d) Credentials Identity

2 Which of the following statements are **false** about Self Sovereign Identity? (you may choose one or more)

i. SSI identity model is based on peer-to-peer relationships between any two entities, and this includes client-server relationships.
ii. The objective of SSI is to empower corporations to control identities and credentials on behalf of individuals in a more secure manner.
iii. SSI identity model is based on peer-to-peer relationships between any two entities, but excludes client-server relationships.
iv. SSI technology provides mechanisms by which credentials can be granted by authorized issuers and then be delivered directly into an entity's SSI wallet.

a) i only
b) i and ii
c) ii and iii
d) ii, iii and iv

3 Which of the following **best describes** a Verifiable Credential?

a) A verifiable credential has four components i.e. ID, Claims, Metadata and Signature of the Issuer.
b) Verifiable implies that the credential can be digitally signed and the digital signature can be cryptographically verified.

c) A VC is a digital and cryptographically secured version of both paper and digital proofs about yourself, like your identity or a qualification you have earned.

d) It can be digitally verified automatically within seconds or even milliseconds, upon request, in a secure and trustworthy way.

4 Fill in the blanks.
The ________________________ is used to represent the interaction among issuers, holders, and verifiers.

a) trust triangle
b) SSI wallet
c) decentralized identifier
d) SSI digital agent

5 Which of the following statements is **true** about SSI Wallets?

a) SSI wallets do not automatically maintain an encrypted backup of the data it manages.
b) SSI wallets are more secure from loss, theft, or hacking than physical wallets.
c) Compared to cloud wallets, the implementation of edge wallets is lightweight and flexible.
d) With edge wallets individuals must rely on a third-party provider to own, control, and manage their own wallet.

6 Which of the following **least describes** a SSI digital agent?

a) It is one of the building blocks of SSI.
b) It uses instructions from its owners, to communicate with other agents over the internet to form connections and exchange credentials.
c) This is a software module in the SSI infrastructure that operates digital wallets on behalf of the owner.
d) It either operates at the edge of the network, if it's an edge agent, or in the cloud if it is a cloud agent.

7 Which of the following statements about decentralized identifiers (DIDs) is **false**?

a) DIDs are just like DNS names which are transferable and human readable.

b) DIDs provide a secure, scalable way for identity holders and their agents to prove ownership of their public keys.

c) DIDs are a type of globally unique identifier or Uniform Resource Identifier

d) DIDs can be permanent and are meant to be machine readable.

8 Complete the following statement.
Governance frameworks ______________________.

a) guide issuers on the policies and procedures that must be followed to issue a credential.

b) uses decentralized networks to avoid single points of failure that PKI infrastructure portends.

c) are specialized cloud service providers.

d) is a part of the Key Management Systems of a digital wallet.

9 Which of the following statements about SSI .features/benefits are **true**? (you may choose one or more)

i. An SSI user agent can make a digitally signed request to other agents for erasure of personal data and later verify if the request was honored.

ii. Using SSI workflow automation, it is possible to achieve a worldwide Business Process Automation (BPA).

iii. A guardianship credential is exactly the same as a delegation credential.

iv. DID based password-less authentication is superior to traditional methods for identity verification and eliminates all prior concerns.

a) iii only

b) i, ii and iv

c) ii, iii and iv
d) All of the above

10 Which of the following **best describes** how SSI RegTech changes the nature of regulation enforcement?

a) The quality of enforcement data is improved.
b) Enforcement actions can be carried out faster.
c) Rules-driven monitoring activity is carried out in real-time, replacing auditing activity conducted after occurrence.
d) The cost of enforcement is substantially reduced.

References

1 Morgan, S. (2015). *IBM's CEO On Hackers: 'Cyber Crime Is The Greatest Threat To Every Company In The World'.* [online] Forbes. Available at: https://www.forbes.com/sites/stevemorgan/2015/11/24/ibms-ceo-on-hackers-cyber-crime-is-the-greatest-threat-to-every-company-in-the-world/.

2 Preukschat, A. and Reed, D. (2021). Why the internet is missing an identity layer—and why SSI can finally provide one. In: *Self-Sovereign Identity: DECENTRALIZED DIGITAL IDENTITY AND VERIFIABLE CREDENTIALS.* Shelter Island: Manning Publications, p.7.

3 Lacity, M.C. and Lupien, S.C. (2022). *Blockchain Fundamentals for Web 3.0.* University of Arkansas Press, pp.56, 57.

4 Reed, D., Preukschat, A. and Hardman, D. (2021). Example scenarios showing how SSI works. In: *Self-Sovereign Identity: DECENTRALIZED DIGITAL IDENTITY AND VERIFIABLE CREDENTIALS.* Shelter Island: Manning Publications, pp.41-44.

5 Lacity, M.C. and Lupien, S.C. (2022). *Blockchain Fundamentals for Web 3.0.* University of Arkansas Press, pp.300, 299, 298.

6 Preukschat, A. and Reed, D. (2021). Why the internet is missing an identity layer—and why SSI can finally provide one. In: *Self-Sovereign Identity: DECENTRALIZED DIGITAL IDENTITY AND VERIFIABLE CREDENTIALS.* Shelter Island: Manning Publications, p.11.

7 Reed, D., Joosten, R. and van Deventer, O. (2021). The basic building blocks of SSI. In: *Self-Sovereign Identity: DECENTRALIZED DIGITAL IDENTITY AND VERIFIABLE CREDENTIALS.* Shelter Island: Manning Publications, pp.21-22.

8 Otto, N., Lee, S., Sletten, B., Burnett , D., Sporny , M. and Ebert, K. (2019). *Verifiable Credentials Use Cases.* [online]

W3.org. Available at: https://www.w3.org/TR/vc-use-cases/ [Accessed 12 May 2025].

9 Hardman, D. (2021). SSI architecture: The big picture. In: *Self-Sovereign Identity: DECENTRALIZED DIGITAL IDENTITY AND VERIFIABLE CREDENTIALS*. Shelter Island: Manning Publications, p.89.

10 Chadwick, D.W. and Burnett, D.C. (2021). Verifiable credentials. In: *Self-Sovereign Identity: Decentralized digital identity and verifiable credentials*. Shelter Island: Manning Publications, p.156.

11 Dock labs (2025). *Self-Sovereign Identity: The Ultimate Guide 2024*. [online] www.dock.io. Available at: https://www.dock.io/post/self-sovereign-identity [Accessed 6 Feb. 2025].

12 Schellinger, B., Sedlmeir, J., Willburger, L., Strüker J. and Urbach, N. (2022): Mythbusting Self-Sovereign Identity (SSI). Discussion paper on digital identities. Branch Business & Information Systems Engineering of Fraunhofer FIT, Bayreuth, p.8.

13 Reed, D., Joosten, R. and van Deventer, O. (2021). The basic building blocks of SSI. In: *Self-Sovereign Identity: DECENTRALIZED DIGITAL IDENTITY AND VERIFIABLE CREDENTIALS*. Shelter Island: Manning Publications, pp. 24-25.

14 Sporny, M., Longley, D. and Chadwick, D. (2019). *Verifiable Credentials Data Model 1.0*. [online] W3.org. Available at: https://www.w3.org/TR/vc-data-model/ [Accessed 14 Apr. 2025].

15 Reed, D., Joosten, R. and van Deventer, O. (2021). The basic building blocks of SSI. In: *Self-Sovereign Identity: DECENTRALIZED DIGITAL IDENTITY AND VERIFIABLE CREDENTIALS*. Shelter Island: Manning Publications, pp. 27-28.

16 Hughes, R. (2020). *Building SSI Digital Wallets: The 3 Major Decisions - Trinsic.* [online] Trinsic -. Available at: https://trinsic.id/ssi-wallets-3-decisions/ [Accessed 12 Feb. 2025].
17 Satybaldy, A., Ferdous, M.S. and Nowostawski, M. (2024). *A taxonomy of challenges for self-sovereign identity systems.* [online] Ieee.org. Available at: https://ieeexplore.ieee.org/stamp/stamp.jsp?arnumber=10413448 [Accessed Feb. 2025].
18 Windley, P. (2023). *Learning Digital Identity.* O'Reilly Media, pp.322, 320.
19 Windley, P. (2023). *Learning Digital Identity.* O'Reilly Media, pp.239-250.
20 Reed, D., Joosten, R. and van Deventer, O. (2021). The basic building blocks of SSI. In: *Self-Sovereign Identity: DECENTRALIZED DIGITAL IDENTITY AND VERIFIABLE CREDENTIALS.* Shelter Island: Manning Publications, pp. 33-34.
21 Vuorenoja, L. (2023). *Getting started with SSI service agent development.* [online] Medium.com. Available at: https://medium.com/@lauravuo/getting-started-with-ssi-service-agent-development-d13c6bccc9c2 [Accessed Feb. 2025].
22 Reed, D., Joosten, R. and van Deventer, O. (2021). The basic building blocks of SSI. In: *Self-Sovereign Identity: DECENTRALIZED DIGITAL IDENTITY AND VERIFIABLE CREDENTIALS.* Shelter Island: Manning Publications, pp. 34-36.
23 Reed, D. and Preukschat, A. (2021). SSI Scorecard: Major features and benefits of SSI. In: *Self-Sovereign Identity: DECENTRALIZED DIGITAL IDENTITY AND VERIFIABLE CREDENTIALS.* Shelter Island: Manning Publications, pp. 59, 63, 65, 68, 73, 80.
24 Reed, D. and Preukschat, A. (2021). SSI Scorecard: Major features and benefits of SSI. In: *Self-Sovereign Identity:*

DECENTRALIZED DIGITAL IDENTITY AND VERIFIABLE CREDENTIALS. Shelter Island: Manning Publications, pp. 59, 63, 65, 68-69, 80.

25 Reed, D. and Preukschat, A. (2021). SSI Scorecard: Major features and benefits of SSI. In: *Self-Sovereign Identity: DECENTRALIZED DIGITAL IDENTITY AND VERIFIABLE CREDENTIALS*. Shelter Island: Manning Publications, p. 65.

26 Reed, D. and Preukschat, A. (2021). SSI Scorecard: Major features and benefits of SSI. In: *Self-Sovereign Identity: DECENTRALIZED DIGITAL IDENTITY AND VERIFIABLE CREDENTIALS*. Shelter Island: Manning Publications, pp. 59, 62, 65, 69-70.

27 Reed, D. and Preukschat, A. (2021). SSI Scorecard: Major features and benefits of SSI. In: *Self-Sovereign Identity: DECENTRALIZED DIGITAL IDENTITY AND VERIFIABLE CREDENTIALS*. Shelter Island: Manning Publications, pp. 60, 62, 69, 72, 77-82.

28 Reed, D. and Preukschat, A. (2021). SSI Scorecard: Major features and benefits of SSI. In: *Self-Sovereign Identity: DECENTRALIZED DIGITAL IDENTITY AND VERIFIABLE CREDENTIALS*. Shelter Island: Manning Publications, pp. 59, 66, 70-71.

29 Ongola, E. (2025). USING BIOMETRICS, BLOCKCHAIN AND SSI TECHNOLOGIES TO COMBAT POST REGISTRATION TRUANCY AND BUDDY PUNCHING. *International Journal of Engineering Applied Sciences and Technology*, 09(12), pp.15–26. doi:https://doi.org/10.33564/ijeast.2025.v09i12.002.

30

9. Suitability of Blockchain

"Truth does not fear investigation. Truth is independent of our opinion"
– Anonymous

9.1 Introduction

By now you know that blockchain is a distributed ledger or a shared data structure. It can also be viewed as a shared database.

At this point you could be wondering whether it would be necessary to replace your current database system(s) with a blockchain. The answer to that important question is "it depends".

It may surprise you to learn that even though blockchain systems design is robust, boasting in-built attributes like redundancy, availability and scalability, they still pale in comparison to many traditional tried and tested database systems such as Oracle and SQL Server, when it comes to performance and latency.

Suffice it to say that implementation of a blockchain system may not necessarily add value in an enterprise, and that traditional databases, including MySQL and Postgres may still be the more viable solution to some data storage problems[1,2].

This chapter takes you through some guidelines on how to determine blockchain's suitability for a given project. To aid in this quest, a student-check-in system is used as an example.

9.2 Student Check-in Overview & Requirements

Student check-ins are conducted for two major reasons. The first one is to try to enforce compulsory education and the second one is to try and bolster performance of individual learners. While not always true[3], it is generally assumed that higher attendance rates positively impacts academic performance[4].

In some countries, student attendance forms the basis for funding of public schools. In other words, government is also interested in student attendance records[5].

The general issues with manual data collection for class attendance are as follows: (1) If the class sizes are large, it can be time consuming for the teacher. (2) Some students might engage in 'buddy punching' if an attendance sheet is being passed around. (3) If the teacher delegates the attendance data collection work, the class representative could be compromised by his/her classmates. (5) Records are easy to modify long after the attendance exercise was conducted. (6) Truancy can be a big concern. (7) If funding is based on attendance, school administrations might present to the government higher numbers than is factual.

A few more considerations are necessary for designing a school attendance system. The first one is that the system would have to be accessible to both schools as well as relevant government education officers. Secondly, because of the first consideration, there should be an access control mechanism that ensures that each school can only manage its own current students' records and government education officials should have "view only" access rights to relevant student records and statistical reports. Lastly, since students might move from one school to another, a national unique student ID is necessary to track a student across the country.

From the above insights, it should be evident why most current implementations of national student records are centralized in nature i.e. there is a master/server computer(s) at a headquarters that hosts a database system which is accessible to schools and relevant government officials via some web application.

Now whereas centralized systems portend a single point of failure, the risks can be mitigated. The bigger issue with a centralized system is with regards to data authenticity and integrity. We cannot be assured that the data we are relying on is accurate, reliable, and authentic because in many cases a systems administrator could tamper with the data.

Could a blockchain system address at least a part of this issue ? (For a more detailed solution read the paper on "Using biometrics, Blockchain and SSI technologies to combat post registration truancy and buddy punching"[6] by Edwin Ongola)

In an attempt to answer this question, the remainder of this chapter uses Pedersen, Risius and Beck's (2019)[7] ten-step decision path for determining the suitability of blockchain technology for a given project.

9.3 Blockchain Suitability for a Student Check-in System

The steps are presented as a series of questions and are summarized in the flowchart in figure 9.1.

Step 1: Is there a need to share a database?
Recall that student attendance records are supposed to be accessible to some government education officers. So for consistency of data, schools would have to share the same database with government education departments.

A blockchain system makes sense when there is a need to share a database.

Step 2: Are there several distinct types of participants?

As alluded to, in step 1, the first party is the school and then the government. In this case we have multiple schools as distinct parties and possibly multiple levels of government education offices, also as distinct parties. In addition we could add parents and the students themselves, as parties.

A blockchain system only makes sense if there are multiple parties (Pedersen, Risius and Beck, 2019, p. 103).

Step 3: Are there conflicts of interest or trust issues among the participants?

There are conflicts of interest because schools are competitors of each other. One school should not have access to records of another school. In addition, schools should not be able to tamper with their own attendance records in order to attract more government funding.

Government should ideally, be able to see only statistical data and not be able to fiddle with figures to justify spending or lack thereof for political reasons.

A blockchain system is appropriate if there are trust issues or conflicts of interest between the parties (Pedersen, Risius and Beck, 2019, p. 104).

Step 4: Do the participants consider a trusted third party undesirable?

If a third party besides schools and government were to be employed to keep student records, there could be considerable trust issues that can emanate from the arrangement. For example, the administrator of the database could be bribed to alter student records.

A blockchain system is appropriate if participants do not want to use a trusted third party.

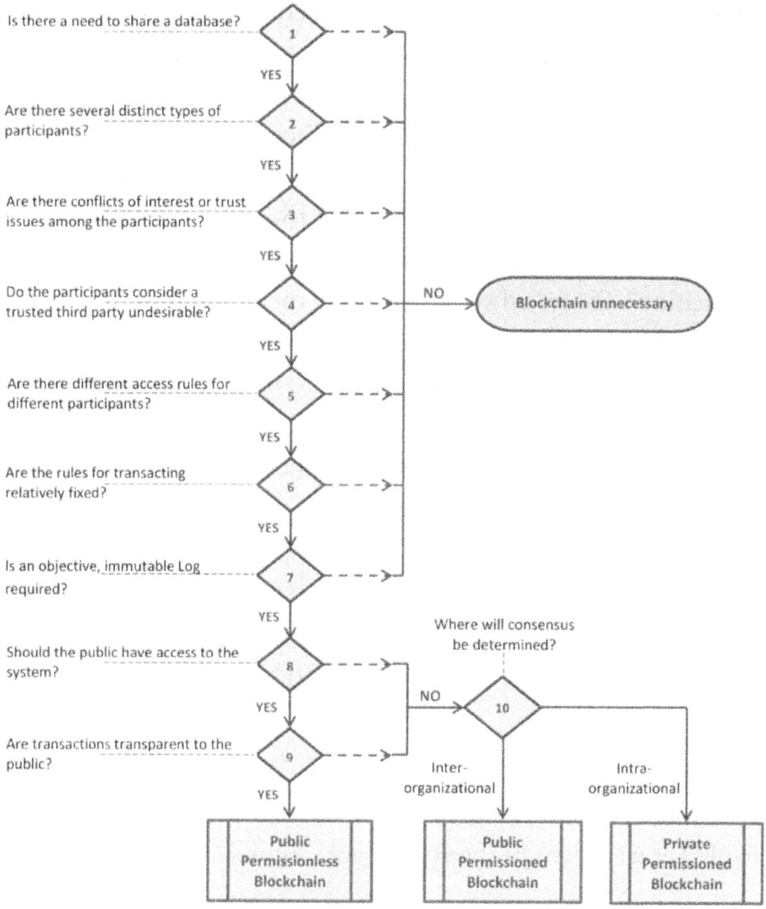

Figure 9.1: Steps for determining the suitability of blockchain in a project[6]

Step 5: Are there different access rules for different participants?

Since attendance records are collected at school level, schools alone should have rights to create new records, but only for their own students. In addition, they will have rights to view attendance records of only their students. All the other parties namely education officers, parents and teachers will have different levels of "read only" rights. Ideally, teachers should only be able to view records for their own classes. Parents should only be able to view records for their children. The school administrator should be able to view all the records of their students and statistical information for their own school. Education officers who are not concerned with children welfare should only be able to view statistical information for any school within their jurisdiction. The officials concerned with children's welfare should be able to see actual records of absentees and their reasons for absence that meet set criteria for "problem students" requiring follow up.

Using blockchain, it is possible to implement an access control mechanism that allows for differing rights for data reading and writing for the different parties in the education ecosystem (Pedersen, Risius and Beck, 2019, p. 107).

Step 6: Are the rules for transacting relatively fixed?

Attendance is straight forward and only the following states are likely for a student in the foreseeable future:

- fully present
- fully absent
- present but came in late and stayed on until end
- came in early and left early
- came in late and left early

- Irregular (was present at the beginning and end of the lesson, but mostly absent in between)

Only the unique codes for the above states, student ID, subject code and time should be stored on the blockchain and this information is highly unlikely to change.

Because the transacting rules are unlikely to change, blockchain technology remains a candidate for this project (Pedersen, Risius and Beck, 2019, p. 108).

Step 7: Is an objective, immutable Log required?

There are cases where individual have certificates for passing certain courses, however, there might be doubt on whether they attended lessons. Generating accurate attendance records would be extremely difficult with a paper based system. It would also be difficult if the student moved from one school to another. But if there is a shared blockchain system among schools, such certificates would be easy to generate using a government issued, unique student id number.

One of the key benefits of any blockchain system is the immutability and integrity of a non-repudiable log of transparent transactions. This tamper proof log would be extremely helpful for auditing student attendance (Pedersen, Risius and Beck, 2019, p. 109).

Note: The steps preceding this one (i.e. Steps 1 to 7), help determine if there is a valid use case for blockchain in a school attendance project. The verdict is yes.

The next steps help us choose the type of blockchain system that we should use for student check-in. Recall that there are private blockchains, public blockchains and consortium blockchains.

Step 8: Should the public have access to the system?

The general public who are not parents would have no interest in accessing a school check-in system. Researchers might be interested, but they can get this information from government education officers or schools, depending on what they are researching. So the general public does not require direct access to this system. This eliminates a public blockchain.

Step 9: Are transactions transparent to the public?

Step 5 and step 8 answer this question to a great extent.

Only education officials, school administrations, teachers and parents would need to read transactions in the system. How about the general public - should they be able to see statistical information about attendance at class, school and different geographical levels ? No, they don't.

Once again, this eliminates a public blockchain leaving us with the option of a consortium blockchain (or public permissioned blockchain) or a private blockchain.

Step 10: Where will consensus be determined?

The validator nodes will check the authenticity of the school making a post, and the validity of the student ID & subject codes used for each record.

It makes sense for the validator nodes to be hosted by both government and schools. Schools hosting validator nodes bring an element of trust that government is not in full control of the network, and therefore long term data integrity can be preserved.

Since parties outside the government are involved i.e. schools and parents, we can also eliminate a private blockchain. Therefore what we end up with is a public permissioned blockchain system run by the government (like a consortium). In this case the public are the schools with delegation rights to their internal staff and parents.

Note: A public blockchain system permissioned by a government has an element of centrality to it, and is against what blockchain systems were intended to do i.e. eliminate dependence on central authorities and middle men.

Conclusion

Blockchain can be a viable solution to business networks that desire a shared view of assets and transactions. Whereas blockchain systems offer benefits such as provenance, security, immutability, consensus, finality, and identity, in certain scenarios, some of these benefits might not be relevant enough to warrant adoption. Other parameters such as network latency and performance may also have to be considered before adoption.

Ultimately blockchain is just a data storage structure and is not panacea for every IT problem. So when considering a blockchain system, one has to examine the business operations and expectations, while paying attention to the participants, the assets and the nature of transactions.

Exercise 9

1. Consider the government's school bursary disbursement system for your country. Briefly explain if and how a blockchain system would help the cause.

____

____

____

____

____

____

____

2. Blockchain based e-voting systems, despite being projected as a credible solution to contentious national elections, have not received the expected uptake around the world. Investigate why and summarize your findings in the space provided below.

____

____

____

____

____

____

3. List any 5 industries that are unlikely to benefit from a blockchain implementation.

i. ______________________________

ii. ______________________________

iii. ______________________________

iv. ______________________________

v. ______________________________

Quiz 9

1 Three of the following attributes are guaranteed on typical blockchain systems. Which one is not?

a) Redundancy
b) Scalability
c) Low network latency
d) Availability

2 Fill in the blanks.
Regular database systems such as ________________________ do better than most blockchain systems, when it comes to performance and latency.

a) Solana and Oracle
b) Bitcoin and Ethereum
c) SQL Server and Bitcoin
d) Oracle and SQL Server

3 Which of the following statements is **true**?

a) A blockchain system makes sense when there is a need to share a database.
b) A blockchain system makes sense when there is a single party involved such as a shop keeper.
c) Blockchain systems are unsuitable for business networks.
d) A blockchain system only makes sense if there is no need to share a database.

4 Which of the following statements are **true** regarding the implementation of blockchain systems? (you may choose one or more)

i. A blockchain system is applicable, when there is a business network with a need to have a shared view of assets and transactions.
ii. A blockchain system is applicable, if there are no conflicts of interest among the parties.

iii. A blockchain system is applicable, if there are no trust issues among the parties.
iv. A blockchain system is applicable, if there are conflicts of interest or trust issues among the parties.

a) i and ii
b) i and iii
c) i and iv
d) ii and iii

5 Which of the following concepts are useful when evaluating a blockchain solution and the benefits it could bring to a network of businesses?

a) Provenance, Immutability and Security
b) Participants, Assets and Transactions
c) Agile programming
d) Redundancy, Availability and Scalability

6 Which of the following **disqualifies** blockchain as a potential solution?

a) Same access rules exist for different participants.
b) High performance and low network latency are NOT critical requirements for business functions.
c) Trusted third parties are undesirable.
d) There is a business network with a requirement to have a shared view of assets and transactions.

7 Complete the following statement.
A blockchain system is applicable when the transacting rules are ____________________ .

a) likely to change
b) determined day to day by the CEO
c) determined by government
d) unlikely to change

8 Which of the following statements is **false**?

a) To determine relevance or usefulness of blockchains in a given industry, we must put into consideration the asset(s) to be tokenized.

b) A blockchain system is applicable, if an objective immutable log is not required.

c) Blockchain system implementations only make sense where there is a network of collaborating parties whose transactions evolve around a shared set of assets in the network.

d) Blockchain systems are not outright replacements for traditional databases.

9 For which of the following industries, would the implementation of blockchain technology be unnecessary or even detrimental? (you may choose one or more)

i. Real Estate
ii. Basic food service
iii. Manual labor services
iv. Supply chain

a) i only
b) i and ii
c) ii and iii
d) ii, iii and iv

10 Fill in the blanks.

We end up with a ______________________________, if consensus is determined within a single organization.

a) public permission-less blockchain
b) private permission-less blockchain
c) private permissioned blockchain
d) public permissioned blockchain

References

1 Bradley, M., Gorman, D., Lucas, M. and Golby-Kirk, M. (2019). *Getting Started with Enterprise Blockchain: A Guide to Design and Development.* 1st ed. USA: O'Reilly, p.20.

2 Greenspan, G. (2015). *Avoiding the pointless blockchain project.* [online] www.multichain.com. Available at: https://www.multichain.com/blog/2015/11/avoiding-pointless-blockchain-project/ [Accessed 8 Sep. 2025].

3 Sekiwu, D. (2020). Investigating the relationship between school attendance and academic performance in universal primary education: The case of Uganda. *African Educational Research Journal,* [online] 8(2), pp.152–160. doi:https://doi.org/10.30918/aerj.82.20.017.

4 OFSTED (1995). *Access, Achievement and Attendance in Secondary Schools* . London: Office of Her Majesty's Chief Inspector of Schools (Ref 16/95/NS).

5 Groginsky, S. (2010). *Student Enrollment Count Mechanisms for School Funding: A Survey of State Policies.* 1580 Lincoln Street, Suite 420 • Denver, CO 80203: Colorado Children's Campaign.

6 Ongola, E. (2025). USING BIOMETRICS, BLOCKCHAIN AND SSI TECHNOLOGIES TO COMBAT POST REGISTRATION TRUANCY AND BUDDY PUNCHING. *International Journal of Engineering Applied Sciences and Technology,* 09(12), pp.15–26. doi:https://doi.org/10.33564/ijeast.2025.v09i12.002.

7 Pedersen, A.B., Risius, M. and Beck, R. (2019). A Ten-Step Decision Path to Determine When to Use Blockchain Technologies. *MIS Quarterly Executive,* 18(2), pp.99–115. doi:https://doi.org/10.17705/2msqe.00010.

10. Current & Future Trends

"There is no security on this earth; there is only opportunity"
- Douglas MacArthur

10.1 Introduction

If you have gone through the last 9 chapters and have also done the exercises, then you have an adequate understanding of what blockchain technology is.

Blockchain's value is such that it is can be used together with other advancing technologies like AI and IoT, to add trust and security to the overall system. Whereas it cannot eliminate all security risks, it has very important elements of data security built in such as integrity, authenticity, immutability and redundancy. Already, blockchain's effect in the financial sector is evident not just from cryptocurrency exchanges, but also from the adoption/accommodation of stablecoins by some financial institutions, and the contemplation of CBDCs by some governments.

But there is more happening away from the financial sector. For example in the food industry, retailers, distributors, processors and farmers are using blockchain, not just to ensure food safety, but to bring about a trust relationship with each other, as well as with the consumer. In this case blockchain is being used to ensure accountability for products from farms to sale outlets. In the healthcare industry, blockchain technology can be used in a similar manner for provenance and to guard against counterfeiting of drugs. If you add in related technologies like SSI, then individuals can be empowered to wield control over their own medical data and be able to share it securely, on a need to know basis[1].

This chapter briefly goes through a few interesting blockchain projects. This includes Machine to Machine Micro Payments, Skill Verification Systems and IDO Launch Platforms. Finally, a few additional projects are mentioned in passing.

10.2 Machine to Machine Micro Payments

Consider a fictitious scenario, where a factory receives raw materials brought by an autonomous agent (a robot of sorts), which is immediately inspected by another autonomous agent, and is then paid for by the receiving agent without human intervention. This is what is referred to as machine to machine (M2M) payments.

In order for this to work, several technologies are involved. Going by our example, the first and obvious technology necessary would be a combination of AI and Robotics. This enables the autonomous agent to move about, identify and even inspect the materials.

The second one is IoT which implies that the autonomous agents should have a clear identity, be embedded with software intelligence, have sensors and most importantly have ubiquitous connectivity to the internet[2]. These autonomous agents must also have support for cryptography because this is a primary method of securing data traversing networks.

The requirement for clear identity invites the third technology, which is SSI. SSI enabled devices are General Data Protection Regulation (GDPR) compliant and can use cryptographic methods to authenticate their identities and address Confidentiality, Integrity and Availability requirements (CIA)[3]. Moreover, using SSI, humans responsible for certain tasks can use delegation credentials to enable autonomous agents to carry out specific parts of the tasks on their behalf.

The fourth technology is Distributed Ledger Technology i.e. blockchain. It would be necessary for recording transactions, and would also be useful in managing identities of autonomous agents. Somewhere in the design, there could be smart contracts that are executed to make payment when the autonomous agent gives the green light.

We talk of M2M payment, but what exactly would the machines be paying each other? The answer lies in the fifth technology that is also based on blockchain i.e. Stablecoins. The allure to stablecoins and not other cryptocurrencies is that, they offer price stability. Stablecoins can facilitate borderless transactions and assist in the movement of money in real time and at very low cost. So stablecoins will likely form part of the foundation for a fully automated machine driven economy.

Some of the sectors that are likely to benefit from M2M payments include manufacturing, logistics and energy[4]. There are also some scenarios where the benefits of M2M payments extend to individuals. For example, consider the automotive industry and picture cars paying unmanned toll stations on freeways and highways. There would be no need for the driver to stop in order to make payment either in cash or via credit card. Instead, the SSI agents of the car and toll station could handle payment. Another place where this same technology would apply is at fuel and e-charging stations, and also at parking facilities[5].

However, for M2M payments to gain widespread adoption there are a number of challenges that need to be overcome. The first one is the complex ecosystem. To make M2M payments a reality, there are many technologies that are involved. There are also many participants with different and sometimes conflicting interests. Then there are also issues to do with regulation, the chief one being that jurisdictions are at different stages of legislation of various rising technologies. Ultimately, standardization of some parts of the M2M ecosystem will be necessary to make seamless interaction possible[6]. A key improvement with regards to scalability is also needed in blockchain technology, the main technology enabling M2M payments. Most blockchain networks, particularly the public ones are known to struggle with high transaction volumes. This must change before M2M payments becomes a commonplace reality.

10.3 Skill Verification System

Technology has made it easier to forge certificates, such that it is common to hear of individuals presenting disputable credentials to recruiters. Shortlisting qualified applicants based on presented documents has been a time consuming exercise and verification of documents has generally been done during the oral interview by people who are probably not equipped to detect forged documents.

However with the advent of blockchain and later SSI technology, the problem of skill verification can be a thing of the past.

Consider a scenario where a government has created an SSI/blockchain infrastructure to handle registration of approved education institutions. These institutions are also SSI/blockchain enabled such that not only have they permanent records of a person's educational and professional accomplishments, but they also offer SSI credentials to their students. If you can recall the discussion on SSI, our Trust Triangle would look as depicted in figure 10.1.

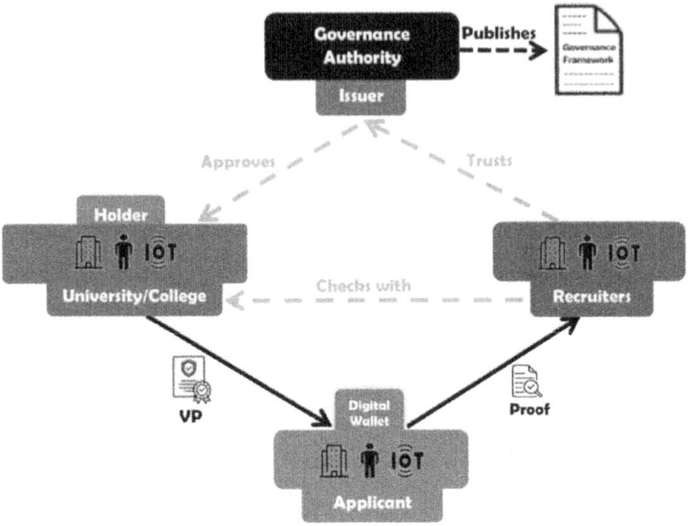

Figure 10.1 Two-sided Trust Triangle for Educational Qualifications

An overview of the procedure an applicant would use when applying for a job posted on a website is as follows:

1. Mary sees an advert for a job that she believes she is qualified for on a website. So she scans the QR code on the application page using the SSI app on her phone.
2. Mary's SSI agent and the recruiter's SSI agent establish a secure communication channel between them that will endure until the recruitment process is over, or either party terminates the connection.
3. Mary's SSI agent sends a Verifiable Presentation (VP) to the recruiter. The VP is like a digital CV and it may be the proof of a combination of different credentials earned from different institutions.
4. The recruiter's SSI agent connects to the government approved education institutions' blockchain and verifies that Mary indeed earned the credentials.

5. The recruiter's SSI agent communicates with Mary's SSI agent and they exchange additional information that qualifies Mary to be invited for an interview.
6. The recruiter's SSI agent sends Mary an invitation letter via email, while Mary's SSI agent marks her calendar and sets up a reminder for her.

Note: The application, verification and invitation take place within a few minutes. (All Mary did was to scan a QR code and her SSI agent used the credentials in her SSI wallet to do the rest).

From the above scenario it should be clear that using SSI/blockchain technology for skills verification would be efficient, accurate, and secure, and thus eliminate certificate fraud.

For recruiters, the system would also lower administrative costs and increase confidence in those who are invited for interviews[7].

Finally, for applicants, a skills verification system based on SSI/blockchain technology simplifies the process and thus encourages more job application attempts. Moreover, because of SSI features like selective disclosure and zero knowledge proofs, applicants' information is not shared unnecessarily and therefore privacy is maintained.

10.4 IDO Launch Platforms

If you did the exercises in the chapters on cryptocurrencies and NFTs, then you might still remember ICOs and STOs. Like the two, Initial Dex Offerings (IDOs) is essentially a crowdfunding method. However, unlike ICOs and STOs, IDOs are decentralized and investors receive tokens directly in exchange for their investment[8].

IDOs primarily serve to democratize investment in blockchain projects. Anyone can participate and since neither a central exchange, nor a central authority exists, the costs of listing are comparatively low. To boost the value of tokens issued, IDOs can be traded immediately, offering instant liquidity.

An IDO Launchpad or launch platform is simply an application on a blockchain system where IDO offerings can be listed. Some of the features of an IDO Launchpad include quick token allocation, integrated wallet, and compatibility with any blockchain technology. Some IDOs may have KYC requirements. Examples of blockchains that have been used as IDO Launchpads include Solana, Cardano and Binnance Smart Chain[9].

Prior to participating in an IDO offering, thorough research on the projects of interest is necessary. Thorough research in this case implies going as far as examining the background of the team behind the project, analyzing the white papers on the project, and also interacting with the communities associated with the project, to gauge the project's chances of success. One practical requirement for all participants is that they should have a crypto wallet that is compatible with the tokens on offer, and they must connect it to their IDO launch platform account. There will be additional platform dependent requirements and policies which each participant must endeavor to be familiar with[8].

After an IDO, investors must monitor both the progress of the project and the performance of the token in the marketplace. The investor's observations will then inform the decision to buy more tokens, or keep the current tokens, or sell some, or sell all.

10.5 Other Blockchain Use cases

Presently there are many ongoing and successful blockchain projects, and new ones still popping up. This section mentions a few in passing.

Charity and Donation Tracking: Some of blockchain's key selling points are immutability, transparency and provenance. Is there a more auditable ledger suitable for tracking donations and expenditure than blockchain?

Indeed organizations like UNICEF[10], Salvation Army[11] and Save the Children[12] have already started accepting donations in crypto. If expenditure is also done in crypto, then there could be some assurance of proper use of money.

Blockchain would also be an excellent tool for tracking disbursement of government school fees bursaries channeled through politicians, because many times the money does not reach the intended beneficiaries.

Blockchain in insurance: Using the idea of parametric insurance and smart contracts, it is possible to do away with filling and verification of claims. To make it even better, policy holders are paid automatically, if an incident concerning them occurs. How would this work?

Consider a client who has a life insurance policy for a loved one. Let say the loved one dies – unfortunately. This information goes to a government public register where all deaths are recorded. This death register serves as an oracle (input) to the insurance claims smart contract on the insurance company's blockchain network. The smart contract just goes through the codified terms (parameters) of the policy and pays out. No claims filing, no investigation and no delays[13].

For this to work properly, insurance companies must work with different arms of government and other industries to establish trust worthy oracles.

AI and Blockchain: Blockchain data being reliable and tamper proof can be used to train AI models for better outcomes. And since the data comes from an immutable ledger, AI's decision making can be audited. Another angle to this is that data belonging to different organizations can be shared to train AI models, while still preserving the privacy of the individual contributors (decentralized training).

One drawback to integrating AI with blockchain is that the latter's limited throughput could hinder AI's real-time capabilities. However, it should be noted that under certain circumstances, AI can in fact be used to improve blockchain's performance by predicting and managing transaction loads.

Examples of industries that can benefit from AI-Blockchain integration are Healthcare, Finance and Supply Chain. In all these industries, blockchain ensures authenticity, integrity and permanence of data. In healthcare, AI will have good data for analysis in order to generate personalized treatment plans for patients. In Supply Chain, AI can use blockchain data to predict potential disruptions. In Finance, AI can use blockchain data to detect anomalies and therefore reduce the risks of fraud.

Two main challenges that could hinder the adoption of AI-Blockchain integration are based on the fact that both fields are relatively new. Consequently, there is lack of standardization and skilled personnel, knowledgeable in both fields. Obviously this will change with time[14].

Blockchain-based sports betting: In the past betting enthusiasts have been limited by bureaucracies in the financial sector. Placing bets using crypto allows an individual to participate in the global market without having to convert to a local currency. There are also no delays when depositing money or withdrawing winnings. Already, there is a large number of organizations offering Blockchain-based sports betting[15]. Some even offer peer to peer (P2P) sports betting. This is only possible because of smart contracts.

10.6 Obstacles to Blockchain Adoption

Whereas blockchain technology has many benefits, its uptake outside the finance related sectors has been comparatively slow. The following are some of the reasons for this state of affairs[16].

1) Limited knowledge and skills

There are people who still cannot tell the difference between bitcoin and blockchain. Some of these are decision makers in organizations that could benefit from blockchain technology.

Even in situations where the management is blockchain literate, engineers, architects, and compliance analysts are still in short supply, thus driving the cost of implementation up.

This will change with time.

2) Regulatory uncertainty

For almost a decade most governments stayed away from cryptocurrencies. Yet for the most of this time, cryptocurrencies were the doorway through which blockchain technology's capabilities could be understood. Some governments went as far as declaring cryptocurrencies illegal. For some people blockchain was and still is synonymous with conmanship. This negatively impacted the attitude of some individuals and organizations towards blockchain, thus slowing down education, investigation and implementations.

This situation appears to be changing since governments around the world have started working on legal frameworks particularly on tokenization. A few have even created their own CBDCs.

3) Functioning legacy systems.

Whereas some organizations can see the potential benefits of blockchain technology, they run legacy systems which currently appear to be serving them well. The cost of an outright upgrade could be prohibitive. Secondly their data might be in a format that does not conform to blockchain technology's decentralized nature, and so integration may be very complicated. Other than that, standard tools for integration may not even exist yet.

In some cases, if it does not disrupt operations, an organization already running a functioning legacy system, can consider upgrading just a part of their system to blockchain initially, and then work towards upgrading the rest later.

Note: Software development requires analysis of the operations and aspirations of the individual company concerned before decisions are made. In some cases generic solutions might not exist.

4) Inability to influence other business network members

As mentioned in chapter 9, blockchain implementations are suitable where there is a business network with a need to have a unified view of resources and the transactions regarding the resources.

It may be possible that only a few members of a business network are interested in implementing blockchain, while the others are reluctant for various reasons.

5) Technological uncertainty

Blockchain technology is heavily dependent on cryptography. Cryptography's security is predicated upon the difficulty and time it would take to unencrypt, say a password, or calculate a private key based a 256-bit public key.

So far, very few entities, if any, have had the kind of resources to engage in this kind of activity. But quantum computing could change everything.

It is expected that in the future, quantum computers will be able to solve in a matter of minutes, what regular computers would take 0.65 quintillion years. What this means is that, if quantum computers are in the wrong hands, blockchains will cease to be immutable and wallets will easily be compromised.

To mitigate this threat scientists are working on **quantum resistance** (or post-quantum cryptography), which are simply cryptographic algorithms and systems that are not vulnerable to attacks using quantum computers[17].

Note: This is more of a concern, rather than a barrier to adoption.

10.7 The Road Ahead

At these early stages of blockchain adoption, many systems are springing up, targeting particular industries or business networks of certain industries. However, in the real world, businesses are interconnected in such a way that a member of one business network may also be a member of other business networks, both local and international. For reflection, think about the supply chain industry. It does not work in isolation, but networks with other sectors such as finance, manufacturing, transportation, and retail.

Already there are attempts to connect the growing number of blockchain networks using blockchain bridges. This might continue until networks and their connections gradually become unwieldy. Eventually a blockchain system might emerge that serves most industries while allowing some element of privacy perhaps through a kind of "one global mainnet with many sidechains" architecture[18, 19].

Conclusion

In summary, blockchain is a distributed ledger technology that can and is changing how some businesses operate across the globe. Because it eliminates middlemen most of the time, this results in business efficiencies and cost reductions. It replaces centralized systems which are a single point of failure. Blockchain has the potential to solve some of the operational problems that governments face.

For both businesses and government, it can help enforce policies and eliminate the need for time consuming, expensive, but error prone audits. However, unless use cases that solve real world problems can be identified, blockchain technology's usefulness would only be for academic purposes.

Be that as it may, blockchain technology is already opening new business opportunities and necessitating reorganization of many others.

Standing in the way of blockchain adoption is the lack of knowledge by leaders, inadequate skilled personnel, standardization that is still maturing, and above all, hesitance fueled by regulations, or the lack of regulation.

Exercise 10

1. Briefly outline the benefits of using blockchain for Intellectual Property Rights Registry.

2. Briefly explain what a mainnet and a sidechain are and describe a scenario where they can be employed.

3. List any 5 differences between ICOs and IDOs.

i.

ii.

iii.

iv.

v.

Quiz 10

1 Which of the following **best represents** the technologies necessary for implementation of M2M payments?

a) IoT, Bitcoin, DLTs and Robotics
b) AI, Robotics, DLTs, IoT, SSI and Stablecoins
c) Blockchain, IoT and Bitcoin
d) AI, Blockchain, IoT and CBDCs

2 Fill in the blanks.
A skills verification system based on SSI/blockchain technology facilitates privacy using features like __________________ and __________________.

a) issuers , verifiers
b) employers , applicants
c) trust triangle, credential wallets
d) selective disclosure, zero knowledge proofs

3 Which of the following statements is **true** regarding Initial Dex Offerings (IDOs)?

a) An IDO is an application on a blockchain system where IDO offerings can be listed.
b) It is not necessary for participants in an IDO to have a crypto wallet that is compatible with IDO tokens.
c) IDO tokens can be traded only after 6 months.
d) IDO is a crowdfunding method meant to democratize investment in blockchain projects.

4 Which of the following is **not** a barrier(s) to adoption of Blockchain Technology? (you may choose one or more)

i. Ability to influence other business network members
ii. Regulatory uncertainty
iii. Post-quantum cryptography
iv. Limited knowledge and shortage of skilled personnel.

a) i only
b) iii only
c) i and iii

d) ii and iv

5 Which of the following is a potential drawback of integrating AI and Blockchain?

a) AI can improve blockchain's performance by predicting and managing transaction loads.
b) Blockchain's limited throughput could hinder AI's real-time capabilities.
c) Decentralized training of AI models can compromise the privacy of the individual contributors.
d) Blockchain improves the quality of data that AI trains on.

6 With regards to blockchain in the insurance industry, which of the following can eliminate the need for filling and verification of claims?

a) Parametric insurance and smart contracts
b) Blockchain bridge and smart contracts
c) Smart contracts and Self Sovereign Identity
d) IoT and parametric insurance

7 Complete the statement.
A blockchain bridge is ______________________________.

a) a service that enables data and assets to be transferred between two different, otherwise isolated, blockchain networks.
b) an independent blockchain linked to a main blockchain
c) another name for SSI DID connection
d) a service that prevents data and assets from been moved between two different, blockchain networks without permission.

8 Which of the following statements is **false** ?

a) Cryptography is heavily dependent on blockchain technology.
b) Quantum computers are expected to be much faster than contemporary computers.

c) In the post-quantum era, security for current blockchain systems could be compromised.

d) Quantum resistance refers to cryptographic algorithms and systems that are not vulnerable to attacks using quantum computers.

9 Which of the following are **true** about differences between ICOs and IDOs? (you may choose one or more)

i. Unlike IDOs that allow immediate buying and selling, ICOs initially have a limited liquidity.
ii. IDO platforms are considered more secure than ICO platforms.
iii. Unlike in ICOs where price is determined by the issuer, IDO prices are determined by market dynamics on the DEX.
iv. Unlike IDOs where transactions occur P2P on decentralized platforms, ICOs occur on centralized platforms like websites and issuers have control over their sales and distribution.

a) ii only
b) i and iii only
c) i, iii and iv only
d) All of the above

10 Which of the following **least describes** side chains?

a) A sidechain is a separate blockchain network that connects to a "parent" blockchain network.
b) Sidechains allow a blockchain network to improve its privacy and security, and minimize the additional trust required to maintain a growing network.
c) A sidechain is what a two-way peg connects.
d) A sidechain is a mechanism by which a blockchain project can expand its ecosystem in a decentralized manner.

References

1 Ashurst, S. and Tempesta, S. (2022). *Blockchain applied : practical technology and use cases of enterprise blockchain for the real world.* Boca Raton, Florida: Routledge, pp.74, 95, 72.

2 Rayes, A. and Salam, S. (2019). *Internet of Things From Hype to Reality The Road to Digitization.* Cham Springer International Publishing, pp.1–2.

3 Sovrin Foundation SSI in IoT Task Force (2020). *Self-Sovereign Identity and IoT.* [online] Sovrin, pp.23–24, 34, 9. Available at: https://sovrin.org/wp-content/uploads/SSI-and-IoT-whitepaper.pdf [Accessed 15 Sep. 2025].

4 Fry, J. (2024). *Digital programmable money enabling machine-to-machine payments.* [online] Medium. Available at: https://medium.com/coinmonks/digital-programmable-money-enabling-machine-to-machine-payments-7ef8564c2bab [Accessed 12 Sep. 2025].

5 Arora, P. (2024). *How M2M Technology Impact The Future of Automotive Finance?* [online] Persistent Systems. Available at: https://www.persistent.com/blogs/machine-to-machine-m2m-payments-a-disruptor-in-automotive-finance/ [Accessed 15 Sep. 2025].

6 Saurabh, S. (2023). *Subex Limited.* [online] Subex. Available at: https://www.subex.com/blog/overcoming-challenges-in-iot-and-m2m-settlements-in-a-b2b2x-scenario/ [Accessed 15 Sep. 2025].

7 Kumar, R.P., Srikanth, K. and Barathi, Dr.B.U.A. (2024). Skill Verification Using Blockchain in a Transparent Future. In: *atlantis-press.com.* [online] International Conference on Computational Innovations and Emerging Trends. Available at: https://www.atlantis-press.com/article/126001945.pdf [Accessed 16 Sep. 2025].

8 Paul, A. (2024). *What is the Difference Between ICO and IDO?* [online] SDLC Corp. Available at: https://sdlccorp.com/post/what-is-ico-and-ido-and-how-

to-participate-here/ [Accessed 16 Sep. 2025].
9 Ajay (2025). *What is IDO Launchpad, and Why Does Blockchain Use It?* [online] SDLC Corp. Available at: https://sdlccorp.com/post/ido-launchpad-and-why-blockchains-used-for-it/ [Accessed 16 Sep. 2025].
10 Lomazzo, C. and Hydary, M. (2020). *The UNICEF CryptoFund.* [online] www.unicef.org. Available at: https://www.unicef.org/innovation/stories/unicef-cryptofund.
11 The Salvation Army (2025). *Donate Cryptocurrency.* [online] The Salvation Army USA. Available at: https://www.salvationarmyusa.org/ways-to-give/donate-cryptocurrency/ [Accessed 17 Sep. 2025].
12 Save the Children (2024). *Donate Bitcoin to Charity.* [online] Save the Children. Available at: https://www.savethechildren.org/us/ways-to-help/donate-bitcoin-to-charity [Accessed 17 Sep. 2025].
13 Hedera (n.d.). *DeFi Insurance: The Next Generation of Insurance.* [online] Hedera. Available at: https://hedera.com/learning/decentralized-finance/defi-insurance [Accessed 17 Sep. 2025].
14 Thanh, D.B. (2025). *The Game-Changing Synergy of AI and Blockchain: Unlocking the Future of Innovation.* [online] SmartDev. Available at: https://smartdev.com/ai-and-blockchain/ [Accessed 17 Sep. 2025].
15 Antier Team (2024). *A Deep Dive into Decentralized Sports Betting Protocols.* [online] Antier Solutions. Available at: https://www.antiersolutions.com/blogs/a-deep-dive-into-decentralized-sports-betting-protocols/ [Accessed 17 Sep. 2025].
16 Brezitska, M. (2025). *Top 6 Blockchain Technology Trends in Various Industries.* [online] binariks.com. Available at: https://binariks.com/blog/emerging-blockchain-technology-trends/ [Accessed 18 Sep. 2025].

17 Hellwig, D., Karlic , G. and Huchzermeier, A. (2020). *Build Your Own Blockchain.* Switzerland: Springer International Publishing, p.163.

18 Bradley, M., Gorman, D., Lucas, M. and Golby-Kirk, M. (2019). *Getting Started with Enterprise Blockchain: A Guide to Design and Development.* 1st ed. USA: O'Reilly, p.71.

19 Roth, S. (2022). *An Introduction to Sidechains.* [online] CoinDesk. Available at: https://www.coindesk.com/learn/an-introduction-to-sidechains [Accessed 18 Sep. 2025].

A final word from the Author

"You may choose to look the other way but you can never again say you did not know"

- William Wilberforce

Congratulations for reaching this far!! I sincerely hope you enjoyed working through the book.

Blockchain Lingo is of an introductory nature, an appetizer of sorts. You are now well equipped to take any direction of interest in terms of further learning in the field of blockchain technology. Whether you want to go into the cryptocurrency space, or enterprise blockchain, or innovative software development, you now have a bird's eye view of what blockchain is about, and can go forth with confidence.

If you read all the chapters, did the exercise and quizzes, then you can no longer claim that you do not know anything about blockchain technology.

I now encourage you to try both the exams, perhaps on different days. Some of the questions in the exams appear deceptively familiar, as if you have encountered them before. You have not. So read them carefully in order not to lose marks unnecessarily. Give yourself approximately 105 mins for each exam. The answers are towards the end of the book. A score of 80% should earn you bragging rights.
Good luck!!!

Edwin Ongola

Exam 1

1. Fill in the blanks.
   A means of exchange should be ________________ enough such that it is not easily obtained without cost.
   a) Plenty
   b) Valuable
   c) Complex
   d) Scarce

2. Which of the following **best portrays** M2M payments?
   a) Toll stations identifying approaching motor vehicles.
   b) Drivers scanning QR codes to pay unmanned toll stations using crypto.
   c) Motor vehicles paying unmanned toll stations on freeways and highways.
   d) Motor vehicles on prepaid subscriptions passing through manned toll stations on freeways and highways without stopping to pay.

3. Which of the following statements is **false**?
   a) The choice made on a database system has no impact on scalability, performance, integrity, storage space, and data privacy.
   b) Database classifications based on deployment could be whether it is centralized, decentralized or distributed.
   c) Decentralized systems are a special type of distributed systems because there is no centralized control.
   d) The decentralized nature of public blockchains means that there is no central administrator(s) to manage the network.

4. Which of the following are **false**? (you may choose one or more)
   i. In a blockchain, the timestamp for when the block was

created is stored in the body section of the same block.

ii. In a blockchain, the timestamp for when the block was created is stored in the header section of the same block.

iii. In a blockchain, the timestamp for each transaction is stored in the header section of the genesis block.

iv. In a blockchain, the timestamp for each transaction is stored in the header section of the same block.

a) i, ii and iii
b) ii, iii, iv
c) ii only
d) i,iii and iv

5. Three of the following attributes are guaranteed on typical blockchain systems. Which one is not?
a) high performance
b) availability
c) redundancy
d) scalability

6. Fill in the blanks.
Using an ____________________ feature on a blockchain, any individual can inspect a DApp's code for assurance of its functionality.
a) off chain
b) oracle
c) on chain
d) decentralized

7. Which of the following is a concern especially for art NFTs?
a) NFT projects will continue perpetually.

b) Intellectual property rights violations when individuals create NFT of other people's work and benefit financially from the same.
c) Impenetrable NFT wallets that cannot be hacked.
d) That regulation will bring about efficiency and considerate taxation.

8. Which of the following statements are **true**? (you may choose one or more)

i. A hashing function is a unidirectional function.

ii. Merkel Trees do not employ any hashing techniques.
iii. A hashing function is an algorithm that takes an input of any size and encrypts it to produce an output of a standard size.
iv. Digital signature forgery becomes possible when there is a hash collision.

a) i, iii and iv
b) iii only
c) ii and iv
d) All of the above

9. Which of the following **best describes** a centralized internet identity model?
   a) In a centralized identity model, accounts are created using user names and passwords.
   b) In a centralized identity model, service providers can sell your data.
   c) A centralized identity model is based on accounts.
   d) In a centralized identity model, a person can create an identity by registering an account with every web application or web service that they intend to use.

10. Which of the following statements is **false**?
    a) Not all contracts that individuals and businesses engage in require lawyers.
    b) The structure of a simple contract can be generalized as "if condition, then no obligation".
    c) Contract disputes can stem from the difficulty in determining whether condition(s) that trigger obligations were met.
    d) The structure of a simple contract can be generalized as "if condition, then action".

11. Complete the following statement.
    The one who studies encrypted information, possibly with the intention of decrypting it is known as a ______.
    a) Cryptographer
    b) Cipher
    c) Cryptanalyst
    d) Kryptós Gráphein

12. Which of the following are **false** regarding web 3.0? (you may choose one or more)

   i. It is also known as the internet of identities.
   ii. It is characterized by collaboration and sharing between users.
   iii. It is also known as the internet of value.
   iv. It is characterized by decentralized networks and users have control over their own data.

   a) i only
   b) ii only
   c) i, iii and iv
   d) None of the above.

13. Which of the following is **not** a configuration item for art NFTs?

   a) Buyer's Trait
   b) Supply
   c) Unlockable content
   d) Ongoing royalty

14. Which of the following **best** describes how smart contracts work?

   a) Smart contracts just carry out all the predefined action(s).
   b) Smart contracts verify conditions and then carry out the predefined action(s) for the prevailing condition.
   c) Smart contracts verify all predefined conditions.
   d) Smart contract actions may generate transactions that change the state of the blockchain.

15. Complete the following statement.
   Both centralized and distributed application systems are usually under the control of ______________________.

   a) validator nodes
   b) a single entity
   c) multiple entities
   d) Miners

16. Which of the following statements is **true** about SSI?

   a) The objective of SSI is to empower corporations to control identities and credentials on behalf of individuals in a more secure manner.

b) SSI technology provides mechanisms by which credentials can be granted by authorized issuers and then be delivered directly into an entity's SSI wallet.
c) SSI identity model is based on peer-to-peer relationships between any two entities, but excludes client-server relationships.
d) Unlike in federated identity model, with SSI, individuals do not have the choice of selective disclosure of personal information.

17. Fill in the blanks.
Regular database systems such as ______________ could be more viable as a solution compared to blockchain systems.
a) Postgres and Litecoin
b) Bitcoin and Ethereum
c) MySQL and Postgres
d) Ethereum and MySQL

18. Which of the following statements are **true**? (you may choose one or more)
i. The original consensus mechanism that was used in Ethereum is Proof of work (PoW).
ii. Proof of work has faster transaction times than Proof of stake (PoS).
iii. Proof-of-Work (PoW) is the latest blockchain network consensus algorithm.
iv. Byzantine Fault Tolerance (BFT) and Proof of Consensus have faster transaction times than Proof of stake (PoS)
a) ii and iii
b) i and iv
c) i only
d) ii, iii and iv

19. Which of the following statements about digital money is **false**?
a) One of the major drawbacks of the first cryptocurrency is that it was a centralized system.
b) bitcoin is not the first cryptocurrency.
c) The original idea of digital money is not Satoshi

Nakamoto's.

d) The primary technology behind Blockchain is Bitcoin.

20. Complete the following statement.
A Verifiable Presentation (VP) to a job recruiter
____.

a) could be a combination of different credentials earned from different institutions.
b) is just another fancy name for a Verifiable Credentials (VC)
c) is a physical CV attested by a lawyer
d) can never contain Zero Knowledge Proof for credentials

21. Which of the following statements regarding STOs are **false**? (you may choose one or more)

i. STO processes do not involve intermediaries such as lawyers.
ii. The security token issuer can interact directly with investors on the designated STO offering platform.
iii. STOs are not limited by geographic borders and are open to more investors over the internet.
iv. A STO issues a security token, which is a digital stock certificate.

a) i only
b) i and ii
c) ii, iii and iv
d) All of the above

22. Which of the following statements **best describes** the ideal preparation prior to participating in an Initial Dex Offering (IDOs)?

a) Acquire a crypto wallet that is compatible with the tokens on offer.
b) Register an account with the relevant IDO launch platform.
c) Join and interact with the communities associated with the project.
d) Analyze the white papers on the project, and examine the background of the team behind the project to gauge the project's chances of success.

23. Which of the following statements is **true**?

i. Block height represents the number of blocks that have been confirmed in the entire history of a particular blockchain network.
ii. The block height of the genesis block is zero.
iii. The tool used to view block information on a blockchain is called a block explorer.
iv. A block explorer can be used to view block height of a particular block.

a) i and iv
b) ii, iii and iv
c) All of the above
d) None of the above

24. Fill in the blanks.
Finality implies that once transactions are committed by ____________________, they cannot be rolled back.

a) immutability
b) blockchain
c) consensus
d) authenticity

25. Which of the following **least describes** Verifiable Credentials?

a) A VC is one of the building blocks of SSI.
b) A VC is a digital and cryptographically secured version of both paper and digital proofs about yourself, like your identity or a qualification you have earned.
c) A verifiable credential has four components i.e. ID, Claims, Metadata and Signature of the Issuer.
d) It can be digitally verified automatically for authenticity or validity within seconds or even milliseconds, upon request, in a secure and trustworthy way.

26. Complete the following statement.
A blockchain system implementation makes sense ______________________________.

a) for solitary businesses.
b) if its performance will not surpass that of SQL Server.
c) when there is a need to share a database.
d) when it is a private blockchain.

27. Which of the following is **not** a problem with the substitution method of encryption?

a) Once an entity has known the encryption/decryption method, they could intercept a message, decrypt, modify it, encrypt it again and send it on its way.

b) The encryption/decryption mechanism does not have to be kept secret.

c) The encryption/decryption mechanism has to be kept secret.

d) The encryption method is so simple that, by repeated guesswork alone, even without a computer, one could infer the actual message from the cipher text.

28. Which of the following **best** describes **b**itcoin from a technical perspective?

a) bitcoin with lower case 'b', is the cryptocurrency, while Bitcoin with capital 'B' refers to the platform.

b) Bitcoin is the first successful cryptocurrency running on a decentralized, peer to peer network.

c) Bitcoin is an immutable, append only, digital distributed ledger that tracks account balances by logging debit and credit transactions.

d) bitcoin is programmable money i.e. a program that has functions for crediting and debiting user balances.

29. Which of the following statements is **false**?

a) Contract law is able to see, ex post, when some obligations are either unfair or unenforceable.

b) The objective of smart contract is to act as an agent of the contracting parties and to actually carry out their obligations on their behalf.

c) Smart contracts can minimize the need for contract litigation in certain scenarios.

d) The objective of contract law is to identify grievances, but not to resolve them.

30. Complete the following statement.
The backend of a DApp is typically coded using languages like ____________________.

a) JavaScript, CSS and HTML

b) COBOL, Visual C++
c) JavaScript, Solidity and HTML
d) Solidity, Vyper, Rust or Golang.

31. Which of the following are **true** regarding cryptocurrency wallets? (you may choose one or more)
   i. Options for storing private keys include paper wallets.
   ii. A wallet address is generated from a private key.
   iii. Transactions are stored inside a wallet only after signing with a private key.
   iv. A wallet address is akin to a bank account number.
   a) i only
   b) i and iv
   c) ii and iii
   d) None of the above

32. Which of the following is a barrier to adoption of Blockchain Technology?
   a) Post-quantum cryptography
   b) Non-functional legacy systems
   c) Regulatory uncertainty
   d) Ability to influence other business network members

33. Which of the following **least describes** NFT marketplaces?
   a) They are like online galleries where one can buy or sell an NFT.
   b) They are like cryptocurrency exchanges, but NFTs are traded for cryptocurrency.
   c) They are like online galleries where one can sell an NFT at a fixed price or auction it.
   d) They are online ecosystems where one can mint an NFT.

34. Which of the following statements are **false** regarding hash collisions? (you may choose one or more)
   i. If a hashing function is not resistant to hash collision, then digital signature forgery becomes possible.
   ii. A good hashing function should not be resistant to hash collision.
   iii. Digital signature forgery is possible even with hash collision due to pre-image resistance.
   iv. Hash collisions occur when several different pre-images

result in the same digest.

a) ii and iii
b) iii only
c) i, ii and iv
d) All of the above.

35. Which of the following statements regarding the implementation of blockchain systems is **false**?

a) A blockchain system is applicable, if there are conflicts of interest or trust issues among the parties.
b) A blockchain system is applicable, when there is a need to share a database.
c) A blockchain system is applicable, if there are no conflicts of interest among the parties.
d) A blockchain system is applicable, when there is a business network with a need to have a shared view of assets and transactions.

36. Which of the following do **not** describe a centralized application? (you may choose one or more)

i. Centralized applications are typically controlled by a single entity.
ii. Centralized applications are typically controlled by many independent entities.
iii. Centralized applications can run on multiple servers but present a single interface to clients.
iv. Centralized applications can run on a single server but present multiple interfaces to the same type of client.

a) ii and iv
b) i only
c) ii, iii and iv
d) All of the above.

37. Which of the following **best describes** non-repudiation?

a) It is enforced by the requirement that transactions be signed using private keys.
b) It is connected to message authenticity.
c) It makes blockchain data more credible.
d) It means that a sender cannot later deny performing a transaction signed using his signature.

38. Fill in the blanks.
A ________________ smart contract never requires information from outside its host blockchain for execution.
a) deterministic
b) ex post
c) non deterministic
d) Oracle

39. Which of the following statements is **true**?
a) Public Blockchain networks are highly decentralized and control is evenly spread among the participating nodes.
b) Public Blockchains are not censorship-resistant and at least one administrator can limit activities of participants.
c) Public Blockchain networks are permission-less and highly decentralized, but not transparent.
d) Public Blockchain networks are transparent, permission-less and centralized.

40. Complete the following statement.
In a basic Trust Triangle, the verifier checks with the
______________________________.
a) Governance framework.
b) Issuer
c) Holder
d) Regulator

41. Which of the following statements are **true**? (you may choose one or more)
i. By design, DApps cannot work with resources within the blockchain network due to technical and trust issues.
ii. An Oracle is like a bridge between the world outside a blockchain and the blockchain itself.
iii. By design, DApps only work with resources within the blockchain network due to technical and trust issues.
iv. A program known as Golang is required so that a DApp can receive information external to its native blockchain network.
a) i and ii
b) iii and iv
c) iv only
d) ii and iii

42. Which of the following statements are **false** with respect to bitcoin mining? (you may choose one or more)

i. The mining block reward on Bitcoin has been fixed since 2009.
ii. Mining using CPUs was unprofitable in 2009.
iii. Mining is an activity currently mostly carried out in mining farms using ASICs, but can be carried out using GPU Rigs albeit with much lower returns.
iv. Mining is the activity used to regulate the supply of bitcoin into the network.

a) i and ii
b) i and iii
c) ii only
d) i, iii, iv

43. Which of the following statements are **false** about SSI Wallets? (you may choose one or more)

i. Compared to cloud wallets, the implementation of edge wallets is lightweight and flexible.
ii. With edge wallets individuals must rely on a third-party provider to own, control, and manage their own wallet.
iii. SSI digital wallet should be implemented using proprietary standards for portability of self-sovereign VCs and other sensitive private data
iv. SSI wallets do not automatically maintain an encrypted backup of the data it manages.

a) i only
b) i,iii and iv
c) ii, iii and iv
d) All of the above

44. Which of the following is an adequate representation of Art NFTs?

a) Enterprise NFTs
b) Collectibles, metaverse assets, trending memes and AI generated art.
c) Videos, 3D models, audios (music), books & prose
d) Virtual worlds on the internet like Decentraland and The Sandbox

45. Which of the following concepts are of **least importance** when evaluating a blockchain solution and the benefits it could bring to a network of businesses?
   a) Participants, Assets and Transactions
   b) Provenance, Immutability and Security
   c) Agile programming, Inheritance and Polymorphism
   d) Redundancy, Availability and Scalability

46. Which of the following is **false** regarding disbandment of blockchain consortia?
   a) A blockchain consortium may be disbanded due to misalignment of incentives among participating companies.
   b) A blockchain consortium may be disbanded because some members might be unable to continue participating due to distraction by business crises.
   c) A blockchain consortium may be disbanded due to alignment of incentives and an excellent business case for participating companies.
   d) A blockchain consortium may be disbanded due to a lack of a compelling business case.

47. Which of the following statements are **true** regarding Merkle trees? (you may choose one or more)
   i. A leaf hash is the hash of a piece of information.
   ii. Merkle root hashes are inputs to leaf hashes.
   iii. Hash tree is another name for Merkle tree.
   iv. Root path begins from the leaf and ends at the root.
   a) i only
   b) iii only
   c) i, iii and iv
   d) ii, iii and iv

48. Complete the following statement.
   A contract deployment transaction is
   ____
   a) the compilation of a smart contract's source code into EVM bytecode.
   b) the transaction that sends the compiled code of a smart contract to the zero address to signify the registration of a new contract on a block chain.

c) the compilation of a smart contract's EVM bytecode into source code.
d) the peer to peer propagation of a smart contract on all nodes of a blockchain network.

49. Fill in the blanks.
The ______________________________ industry primarily uses blockchain for provenance tracking.
a) supply chain
b) medical
c) banking and finance
d) education

50. Which of the following statements is **true** regarding integrating AI and Blockchain?
a) Blockchain has the potential to improve the quality of data that AI trains on.
b) Blockchain's performance cannot be improved by AI.
c) Blockchain's limited throughput is best for AI's real-time capabilities.
d) Decentralized training of AI models always compromises the privacy of the individual contributors.

51. Which of the following statements are **true** regarding NFTs? (you may choose one or more)
i. Creating NFTs to represent trustworthy scientific papers can help in reducing plagiarism.
ii. In terms of market valuation, it is enterprise NFTs that currently dominates, compared to NFTs from rare prestige art.
iii. NFTs cannot be used to represent official documents like national IDs.
iv. NFTs can be used to facilitate fractional ownership of expensive assets such as real estate, aircrafts or yachts.
a) iii only
b) ii and iii
c) i, ii and iv
d) i and iv

52. Which of the following statements are **false** about SSI digital agents? (you may choose one or more)

i. These are hardware modules in the SSI infrastructure that operate digital wallets on behalf of their owners.
ii. They are one of the building blocks of SSI.
iii. Cloud agents operate on an identity holder's local devices.
iv. They use instructions from their owners, to communicate with other agents over the internet to form connections and exchange credentials.

a) i and iii
b) ii and iv
c) ii, iii and iv
d) None of the above

53. Which of the following describes the property of "soundness" in Zero Knowledge Proof Systems?
a) If the statement is true, no verifying party can learn anything besides the fact that the statement is true.
b) If the statement is false, no dishonest party (prover) can convince honest verifiers.
c) If the statement is false, no verifying party learns anything besides the fact that the statement is true.
d) If the statement is true, an honest verifying party will be convinced by an honest prover.

54. Complete the following statement.
When a blockchain project that involves the use of a native cryptocurrency is a potential solution to significant problem(s) for a large section of the society, we can say that the cryptocurrency has ______________________.
a) speculative value
b) rising value
c) utility value
d) altcoin use cases

55. Which of the following statements are **false**? (you may choose one or more)
i. Oracles are necessary for non-deterministic smart contracts to improve their quality of decision making.
ii. All consumers have the competence and the required knowledge to influence smart contract operations.
iii. Smart contracts are typically used in business transaction scenarios that target a large number of customers.

iv. In conformity with trustless systems, smart contracts, require trust between the parties, and external monitoring of contractual obligations or enforcement.

a) i only
b) iv only
c) ii and iv
d) i and iii

56. Which of the following **disqualifies** blockchain as a potential solution?

a) High performance and low network latency are NOT critical requirements for business functions.
b) Different access rules exist for different participants.
c) There is a business network with a requirement to have a shared view of assets and transactions.
d) Trusted third parties are desirable.

57. Which of the following statements is a **true** description of a blockchain bridge?

a) It is an independent blockchain linked to a main blockchain.
b) It is a service that facilitates the movement of data and assets between two different, otherwise isolated, blockchain networks.
c) It is a program that prevents data and assets from being moved between two different, blockchain networks without permission.
d) It is another name for SSI DID connection.

58. Complete the following statement.
A distributed application system ____________________

a) presents itself to clients like a single system, even though it could be spread across two or more networked computers.
b) is another name for a centralized system.
c) is another name for a decentralized system.
d) presents itself to clients like multiple systems, even though it is installed on just one single central server.

59. Which of the following statements is **false**?

a) The government is likely to be attracted to blockchain

due to its identity management benefits.

b) Media and Entertainment industry is likely to be attracted to blockchain due to its disintermediation benefits.

c) The supply chain industry is most likely attracted to blockchain due to its user identity management benefits.

d) The insurance industry is likely to be attracted to blockchain due its process automation capabilities using smart contracts.

60. Which of the following statements are **false**? (you may choose one or more)

i. Private-permissioned blockchains limit the number of nodes needed to validate transactions.

ii. Most enterprise blockchain solutions are unlikely to be private-permissioned blockchains.

iii. Private blockchains are also known as permission-less blockchains.

iv. The allure to private-permissioned blockchains is that they provide assurances of resource efficiency, fast settlement times, confidentiality, and regulatory compliance.

a) i and iv

b) iii only

c) i only

d) ii and iii

61. Which of the following statements are **true** regarding the impact of blockchain technologies in the Media and Entertainment industry? (you may choose one or more)

i. Creators can receive royalty payments directly.

ii. Using smart contracts and NFTs, counterfeiting of digital products can be reduced.

iii. Artists can receive more favorable income.

iv. Creators are enabled to interact directly with their customers or fans.

a) i and ii only

b) ii and iv only

c) i, iii and iv only

d) All of the above

62. Complete the following statement.

In solidity, smart contract methods are called ____________________.

a) encapsulation
b) procedures
c) classes
d) functions

63. Which of the following statements is **false** about blockchain forks?

a) A blockchain fork can be intentional or unintentional.
b) A blockchain hard fork requires all nodes or users who wish to remain on the old chain to downgrade to the original version of the software.
c) A soft fork is a backwards-compatible, intentional change to a blockchain's consensus mechanism.
d) Soft forks do not split a chain, because the old and new rules are compatible with the system function.

64. Which of the following statements is **true**?

a) On the Ethereum network, the general standard for NFTs is ERC-725.
b) On the Ethereum network, the NFT standard for identity claims is ERC-721.
c) On the Ethereum network, the general standard for NFTs is ERC-721.
d) On the Ethereum network, the NFT standard for collectibles is ERC-721.

65. Which of the following describes a decentralized application system?

a) A decentralized application is replicated in its entirety, on each node of a blockchain network.
b) A decentralized application on a blockchain is a black box, since it is impossible to inspect its source code.
c) A decentralized application is a misnomer, since it is installed only on the main server of a blockchain network.
d) A decentralized application is one that cannot be replicated, which makes it unique and this drives up its price.

66. Which of the following are **false** regarding blockchain implementations? (you may choose one or more)

i. A blockchain system is applicable when trusted third parties are undesirable.
ii. A blockchain system is applicable when the transacting rules are likely to change.
iii. A blockchain system is applicable when high performance and low network latency are not critical success factors.
iv. A blockchain system is applicable when there is a need to share a database.

a) ii only
b) ii and iii
c) i, iii and iv
d) All of the above

67. Which of the following are **false** about stablecoins? (you may choose one or more)

i. Stablecoins are mostly used to facilitate trading across different cryptocurrency exchanges.
ii. Stablecoins are non-fungible.
iii. Algorithmic stablecoins are backed by commodities like gold, oil, diamonds etc.
iv. Stablecoins pegged 1:1 to a cryptocurrency are not likely to be subject to the price volatility of that cryptocurrency.

a) i only
b) iii only
c) ii, iii and iv
d) All of the above

68. Which of the following statements about SSI decentralized identifiers (DIDs) are **true**? (you may choose one or more)

i. DIDs can be permanent and are meant to be machine readable.
ii. DIDs are similar to DNS names only to the extent that both are globally unique.
iii. Peer DIDs do not require the use of any external database.
iv. DIDs make use of asymmetric-key cryptography.

a) i only
b) i, iii, iv
c) None of the above

d) All of the above

69. Complete the following statement.
When a hashing algorithm cannot infer from the current input, a second pre-image that results in the same digest, we say that is ______________________.
a) second hash value resistant
b) second pre-image resistant
c) second collision resistant
d) pre-image resistant

70. With regards to P2P sports betting which of the following is **false**?
a) There could be regulatory uncertainty due to the decentralized and international nature.
b) It is less transparent than traditional sports betting.
c) Participants can bet for or against an event outcome.
d) Bets might not be matched instantly.

71. Which of the following does **not** describe Digital signatures?
a) Digital signing implies transforming a message using a private key and then sending the result together with the message to a receiver who can verify it.
b) In digital signing, a sender signs a message with his public key and the recipient later decrypts it with the sender's private.
c) A message that has been transformed using a private key is called a digital signature.
d) In digital signing, a sender signs a message with his private key and the recipient later decrypts it with the sender's public.

72. Which of the following statements is **true**?
a) Cryptography is heavily dependent on blockchain technology.
b) In the pre-quantum era, security for current blockchain systems could be compromised.
c) Quantum computers are expected to be much slower than contemporary computers.
d) Quantum resistance refers to cryptographic algorithms and systems that are not vulnerable to attacks using

quantum computers.

73. Which of the following is **false** regarding privacy coins (Monero)?
   a) Wallet addresses on Monero are considered 'pseudoanonymous'.
   b) Monero employs ring signatures to solve the privacy problem.
   c) Monero's PoW algorithm is ASIC resistant.
   d) The concern on privacy coins is that they could be used to facilitate illegal activities.

74. Fill in the blanks.
   A blockchain system implementation is applicable, if ______________________________ is required.
   a) low network latency
   b) solitary business operation
   c) an objective immutable log
   d) very high performance

75. Which of the following **best describes** the benefits of blockchain networks?
   a) Efficiency, speed and consortium networks.
   b) Smart contracts and NFTs.
   c) Tamper resistance and cryptography.
   d) Fault tolerance, provenance and immutability.

76. Which of the following statement about security tokens are **true?** (you may choose one or more)
   i. Security token can facilitate fractional ownership and thus increase liquidity in traditionally illiquid markets.
   ii. Security tokens can be used to represent physical or digital assets.
   iii. Unlike fungible tokens, security tokens are not recorded on a blockchain.
   iv. Security tokens are synonymous with certificates of ownership and authenticity.
   a) i only
   b) iii only
   c) i, ii and iv
   d) ii, iii and iv

77. Complete the following statement.
Governance frameworks ________________________.

a) use decentralized networks to avoid single points of failure that PKI infrastructure portends.
b) is a set of business, legal, and technical rules created and administered by an entity known as the governance authority.
c) is a part of the Key Management Systems of a digital wallet.
d) specify only what a governance authority can or cannot do.

78. Which of the following statements are **false**? (you may choose one or more)

i. The first functional or successful blockchain network is the Bitcoin network.
ii. DApps cannot take advantage of the inherent benefits of blockchain networks such as immutability, security and resilience.
iii. The native cryptocurrency on the Ethereum blockchain network is called Ether.
iv. Ethereum network was intended primarily for transferring ether (cryptocurrency) from one account to another.

a) All of the above
b) i and ii only
c) ii, iii and iv
d) ii and iv only

79. Which of the following is an **unlikely** blockchain technology use case in the government sector?

a) Cryptocurrency trading
b) Identity management
c) Transparency and accountability
d) Research

80. Which of the following statements are **false**? (you may choose one or more)

i. Transactions sent to smart contract addresses may contain only crypto as parameters.
ii. Smart contract generated transactions cannot change the

state of the blockchain.

iii. Smart contracts are similar to Standard Contract Forms.

iv. Decentralized Autonomous Organizations are not smart contacts.

a) ii only
b) i and ii
c) ii, iii and iv
d) i, ii and iv

81. Which of the following statements is **false**?

a) Provenance on a blockchain structure is made possible through cryptography.
b) Blockchain technology reliance on cryptography makes it immutable.
c) Blockchain technology's decentralized nature makes it fault tolerant.
d) With blockchain technology, one cannot get a complete audit trail of transaction concerning a given entity or object.

82. In which of the following group of industries, would the implementation of blockchain technology be unnecessary or even detrimental?

a) Traditional hairdressing, small-scale agriculture with local customers, and manual labor services.
b) Health care, Real estate, and Education
c) Supply chain, Oil & Gas, and Education
d) Basic food service, Supply chain and Real estate

83. Which of the following statements is **true**?

a) Token standards are the same across all blockchains.
b) An NFT is a physical asset whose ownership is recorded on a blockchain.
c) An NFT is a digital asset whose ownership is recorded on a centralized system.
d) A blockchain is only required for the transfer and storage of NFT information.

84. Fill in the blanks.

____________________ is an online editor that can be used to write the programming logic for Ethereum DApps before compiling them.

a) Atom
b) Remix
c) Solidity
d) CSS

85. Which of the following statements **does not** describe a SSI feature or benefit?

a) Using guardianship credentials, an entity can operate SSI agents and wallets on behalf of another entity.
b) A delegation credential is exactly the same as a guardianship credential.
c) Using SSI workflow automation, it is possible to achieve a worldwide Business Process Automation (BPA).
d) Using DID-based password less authentication, all concerns regarding traditional identity verification methods are eliminated.

86. Which of the following statements is **false** about ICOs?

a) Prior to an ICO, startup founders are not always subjected to thorough background checks.
b) Prior to an ICO, the concerned startup is not always required to register with a government regulatory agency.
c) After an ICO, a startup is required to provide financial statements as well as business updates to the public investors.
d) Coins issued at an ICO are traded at cryptocurrency exchanges, which are not all subject to regulation.

87. Which of the following statements are **true**? (you may choose one or more)

i. Smart contracts' functionality is unpredictable, but transparent.
ii. Smart contracts cannot lower the risk of collaboration.
iii. Smart contracts are trustless systems.
iv. Smart contracts unlike transactions on blockchains are not immutable.

a) iii only
b) i and iii
c) i, ii and iv
d) i, iii and iv

88. Which of the following statements is **true**?
a) Another term for digest is pre-image.
b) The output to a pre-image is called the hashing functionality.
c) The input to a hashing function is called the digest.
d) Pre-image resistance implies that, even using computational brute force it is difficult to determine the pre-image from the resulting hash value.

89. Fill in the blanks.
A sidechain is a _________ blockchain network that connects to a "_________" blockchain network.
a) twin, child
b) separate, parent
c) child, twin
d) separate, child

90. Complete the following statement.
Blockchain technology can be used in a decentralized energy production ecosystem to track
______________________________.
a) temperature and consumption
b) integrity and authenticity
c) consumption and payments
d) temperature and production

91. Which of the following statements has been offered by Central banks as a reason for considering the implementation of CBDCs ?
a) To facilitate surveillance capitalism.
b) To streamline international trade finance and to reduce dependency on the dollar.
c) To punish dissent.
d) To totally control their citizens finances and assets, and consequently, to control their behavior.

92. Which of the following are **true** regarding encryption methods? (you may choose one or more)
i. Public key cryptography is an example of asymmetric encryption.

ii. In symmetric encryption, the sender and receiver do not use the same keys for encryption and decryption.
iii. A message encrypted using a private key must also be decrypted using the same private key to achieve confidentiality.
iv. Secure transmission of the decryption key to the sender, is a problem in symmetric encryption.

a) i only
b) ii, iii and iv
c) i and iv
d) ii and iii

93. Which of the following statements is **false** regarding smart contracts' shortcomings?

a) Smart contracts are on the verge of replacing contract law.
b) Only a small subset of users might be in a position to truly understand a smart contract's code in order to verify its functionality.
c) Under certain scenarios smart contracts' transactions can still lead to legal disputes.
d) Smart contracts are unable to give any consideration to new developments that its designers/programmers had not taken into account.

94. Three of the following statements are advantages of SSI RegTech. Which one is not ?

a) Rules-driven monitoring activity is carried out after occurrence.
b) The cost of enforcement is substantially reduced.
c) Enforcement actions can be carried out faster.
d) The quality of enforcement data is improved.

95. Fill in the blanks.
Unlike ICOs that initially have a ____________, IDOs allow immediate buying and selling.

a) limited liquidity
b) centralized platform
c) less secure platform
d) unlimited liquidity

96. Which of the following **best** describes a decentralized application?

a) A DApp is a distributed application that is built on top of open, decentralized, client-server infrastructure services.
b) A DApp is a decentralized cryptocurrency wallet.
c) A DApp is a web application that is built on top of open, decentralized, P2P infrastructure services.
d) A DApp is a decentralized DeFi application.

97. Complete the following statement.
If consensus is determined across a number of member organizations, we end up with a ______________________.

a) public permission-less blockchain
b) private permission-less blockchain
c) private permissioned blockchain
d) public permissioned blockchain

98. Which of the following is **not true** about censorship resistance?

a) It is the ability of blockchain network to resist attempts to secure all transactions within a network from potential meddling, thus making it immutable.
b) It is the ability of blockchain network to resist attempts to censor, alter or stop the flow of information.
c) It creates an environment where activities cannot be unjustly blocked, scrutinized, or manipulated by authorities and other adversaries.
d) It ensures that all transactions within a network are secured from potential meddling, thus making it immutable.

99. Complete the following statement.
All of the following are fungible except ______________.

a) Japanese Yen
b) fiat currency
c) Ethereum
d) digital collectibles

100. Fill in the blanks.
In the education sector, blockchain technology can mostly be

useful for ______________, ______________ and ______________.

a) disintermediation, production tracking , P2P betting
b) record keeping, policy issuance, micro payouts tracking
c) consumption tracking , claims verification, data publishing
d) identity management , record keeping, verification of credentials

Final Exam 2

1. Fill in the blanks.
   Database classification based on deployment could be whether it is __________, _________ or _____________.
   a) hierarchical, network, relational
   b) centralized, distributed, decentralized
   c) blockchain, NoSQL, relational
   d) object-oriented

2. Which of the following is the **key reason** for the preference of stablecoins in M2M payments?
   a) They facilitate borderless transactions.
   b) They assist in the movement of money in real time.
   c) They offer price stability.
   d) They have very low transaction costs.

3. Which of the following statements is **false**?
   a) The input to a hashing function is called a digest.
   b) Digital signature forgery becomes possible when there is a hash collision.
   c) Hashing functions are "one way" functions.
   d) Both digital signatures and Merkel trees employ hashing functions.

4. Which of the following are **not** concerns regarding NFTs? (you may choose one or more)
   i. Intellectual property rights violations when individuals create NFT of other people's work and benefit financially from the same.
   ii. NFT projects will continue perpetually.
   iii. Regulation will bring about efficiency and considerate taxation.
   iv. An NFT owner's wallet could be hacked, leading to the theft of his NFTs.
   a) i and ii
   b) ii and iii
   c) i, ii and iii

d) ii, iii and iv

5. Which of the following **least describes** the federated identity model?
   a) It is what companies like Facebook, Google, Amazon and LinkedIn do about logging in.
   b) The federated identity model increases institutional power over users' data and sometimes, they monetize user data for their own advantage.
   c) The federated identity model is more convenient for users in terms of password management than the centralized model.
   d) In the federated identity model, organizations invite users to access multiple sites through a single account managed by them.

6. Complete the following statement.
   A decentralized application is ____________________
   a) installed only on the main server of a blockchain network.
   b) exactly like a distributed system.
   c) not created to leverage on the advantages of a blockchain network.
   d) replicated in its entirety, on each node of a blockchain network.

7. Which of the following statements is **true**?
   a) Attributes like high performance and scalability are guaranteed on blockchain systems.
   b) Attributes like high performance and low network latency are not guaranteed on blockchain systems.
   c) Attributes like low network latency and scalability are guaranteed on blockchain systems.
   d) Attributes like scalability and availability are not guaranteed on blockchain systems.

8. Which of the following statements are **true** regarding means of exchange? (you may choose one or more)
   i. It should be able to serve as a store of value.
   ii. It should be bulky if it has any real value just like gold.
   iii. It should be scarce enough such that it is not easily

obtained without cost.

iv. It should have units of account.

a) i, ii and iii
b) i and iv only
c) i, iii and iv
d) ii, iii and iv

9. Which of the following **best describes** the purpose of a consensus mechanism in a blockchain network?
   a) They make sure that the data that is recorded on the transaction ledger is not subjected to a 51% attack.
   b) They make sure that the data that is recorded on the transaction ledger is valid and up-to date and that, each of the nodes on the blockchain network has a unique ledger.
   c) They make sure that when a 51% attack occurs, the entire system automatically defaults to Proof of Stake (PoS) mechanism.
   d) They make sure that the data that is recorded on the transaction ledger is valid and up-to date and that, all the nodes on the blockchain network are synchronized.

10. Fill in the blanks.
   The structure of a simple contract can be generalized as "if ________________, then action".
   a) no obligation(s)
   b) action(s)
   c) condition(s)
   d) smart contract

11. Which of the following statements about digital money is **false**?
   a) The primary technology behind Bitcoin is Blockchain.
   b) The original idea of digital money is not Satoshi Nakamoto's.
   c) bitcoin is the first cryptocurrency.
   d) One of the major drawbacks of the first cryptocurrency is that it was a centralized system.

12. Which of the following statements are **false** regarding web 3.0? (you may choose one or more)
   i. It is also known as the internet of identities.

ii. It is characterized by applications such as Facebook (Meta), WhatsApp and YouTube.
iii. It is characterized by decentralized networks and users can have control over their own data.
iv. It is characterized by collaboration and sharing between users.

a) i and iii
b) i, ii and iii
c) ii, iii and iv
d) ii and iv

13. Which configuration item can be used to control the total number of NFTs that can be minted for a given project?
    a) Unlockable content
    b) Number of Perks
    c) Number of Traits
    d) Supply

14. Which of the following **best describes** a block timestamp?
    a) This is the data stored in each block, within the header section, that indicates the exact moment that the block was created.
    b) This is the set of transactions stored in each block, within the header section, that indicates the exact moment that the last transaction in the block was completed.
    c) This is the data stored in each block, within the header section, that indicates the exact moment that the previous block was created.
    d) This is the data stored in each block, within the body section that indicates the exact moment that the block was created.

15. Complete the following statement.
    A Verifiable Presentation (VP) to a job recruiter ______________________.
    a) can never be a combination of VCs or combination of parts of VCs.
    b) is just another fancy name for a VCs
    c) can contain Zero Knowledge Proof for some credentials
    d) is a digital CV attested by a lawyer

16. Which of the following statements is **true**?
   a) Smart contract actions never generate transactions that change the state of the blockchain.
   b) Smart contracts verify conditions and then carry out the predefined action(s) for the prevailing condition.
   c) Smart contracts are duplicated on some of the nodes of a blockchain.
   d) Smart contracts verify conditions and but do not carry out the predefined action(s) for the prevailing condition.

17. Complete the following statement.
   Cipher is another term for ________________________.
   a) Cryptanalyst
   b) encryption
   c) cryptographer
   d) decryption

18. Which of the following statements is **true** regarding blockchain performance and latency? (you may choose one or more)
   i. Bitcoin does better than SQL Server.
   ii. Oracle does better than most blockchain systems.
   iii. Bitcoin does better than Oracle.
   iv. SQL Server does better than most blockchain systems.
   a) i only
   b) ii and iv
   c) iii and iv
   d) ii, iii and iv

19. Which of the following statements concerning SSI is **false**?
   a) SSI identity model is based on peer-to-peer relationships between any two entities, and this includes client-server relationships.
   b) SSI technology provides mechanisms by which credentials can be granted by authorized issuers and then be delivered directly into an entity's SSI wallet.
   c) SSI is a set of technologies that encompasses Identity Management, distributed ledger technology (Blockchain), cryptography, and distributed computing.
   d) Unlike in federated identity model, with SSI, individuals do not have the choice of selective disclosure of personal information.

20. Complete the following statement.
Using an on chain feature on a blockchain, any individual can ______________________________

a) improve a DApp's code for better functionality.
b) delete a DApp's source code to stop it from functioning.
c) inspect a DApp's code for assurance of its functionality.
d) connect to any oracle for off chain data.

21. Which of the following are **not** reasons for companies to join a blockchain consortium?

i. To build a critical mass of adoption
ii. To achieve cost savings
iii. To influence standards
iv. To accelerate learning
v. To share risks
vi. To maintain relevance

a) None of the above
b) iii and vi
c) i, ii, iv and v
d) All of the above

22. Which of the following lists **best** represents blockchain's key benefits?

a) Consensus, finality, immutability and provenance
b) Integrity, authenticity and non-repudiation
c) Availability, redundancy and security
d) Smart contracts

23. Which of the following statements regarding STOs is **true**?

a) STOs are limited by geographic borders and are not open to more investors over the internet.
b) The security token issuer never interacts directly with investors on the designated STO offering platform.
c) A STO issues a security token, which is a digital stock certificate.
d) STO processes do not involve intermediaries such as lawyers.

24. Fill in the blanks.
Technically, in cryptocurrency blockchains, ____________ carry

data about debits and credits, not digital currency.

a) wallets
b) public keys
c) transactions
d) oracles

25. Which of the following is **not** a characteristic of distributed application systems?
  a) In comparison to centralized application systems, distributed applications are harder to administer.
  b) Distributed application systems appear to clients like a single system, yet it could be spread across two or more networked computers, working together to provide a required service.
  c) In comparison to centralized application systems, distributed applications are easier to secure.
  d) In a distributed system, the clients need to trust the service provider.

26. Complete the following statement.
  A blockchain system implementation makes sense
  ____________________________________.
  a) when it is a public blockchain.
  b) when there is a need to share a database.
  c) if its performance will not surpass that of Oracle.
  d) for solitary run businesses like shops.

27. Which of the following **best describes** a Verifiable Credential?
  a) Verifiable implies that the credential can be digitally signed and the digital signature can be cryptographically verified.
  b) A VC is one of the building blocks of SSI.
  c) A verifiable credential has four components i.e. ID, Claims, Metadata and Signature of the Issuer.
  d) A VC is a digital and cryptographically secured version of both paper and digital proofs about yourself, like your identity or a qualification you have earned.

28. Which of the following describes hash collisions?
  a) Hash collisions occur when successful determination of the pre-image can be made from the resulting digest,

using computational brute force.

b) Hash collisions occur when a proof of the hash is provided instead of the hash itself.

c) Hash collisions occur because hashing functions are inherently one to many functions.

d) Hash collisions occur when two or more pre-images result in the same digest.

29. Which of the following statements is **false**?

a) Smart contracts can minimize the need for contract litigation in certain scenarios.

b) Contract law is able to see, ex post, when some obligations are either unfair or unenforceable.

c) The objective of contract law is to identify grievances and to resolve them.

d) The objective of smart contract is to act as an agent of the contracting parties, but not to actually carry out their obligations on their behalf.

30. Fill in the blanks.

After an Initial Dex Offering (IDO), investors should ____________ and ______________.

a) read the white papers on the project, examine the background of the team behind the project

b) monitor the progress of the project, monitor the performance of the token in the marketplace

c) monitor the progress of the project, examine the background of the team behind the project

d) read the white papers on the project, monitor the performance of the token in the marketplace

31. Which of the following statements are **true** about NFT marketplaces? (you may choose one or more)

i. All NFT marketplaces are decentralized.

ii. Some NFT marketplaces require pre-approval before being allowed to list NFTs for sale, while others do not.

iii. NFT marketplaces are like cryptocurrency exchanges, but here NFTs are traded for cryptocurrency.

iv. Some NFT marketplaces are very specialized in that they list a very specific type of NFT only, while others are more generalized.

a) i only
b) ii and iv only
c) ii, iii and iv
d) All of the above

32. Which of the following is **true** regarding the implementation of blockchain systems?
   a) A blockchain system is applicable, if there are no conflicts of interest among the parties.
   b) A blockchain system is applicable, when there is a business network with a need to have a shared view of assets and transactions.
   c) A blockchain system is applicable, if there are no trust issues among the parties.
   d) A blockchain system is applicable, when the need to share a database does not exist.

33. Which of the following **does not describe** a public blockchain?
   a) A public blockchain is a permission-less network, where any participant can upload data to the ledger and the data can be viewed by anyone.
   b) Public Blockchain networks are highly decentralized, permission-less, censorship-resistant, trustless and transparent.
   c) A public blockchain is a permissioned network that is trustless and transparent.
   d) Public Blockchain networks are highly decentralized and control is evenly spread among the participating nodes.

34. Which of the following statements are **false**? (you may choose one or more)
   i. A non-deterministic smart contract never requires information from outside its host blockchain for execution.
   ii. A deterministic smart contract is one that requires information from outside its host blockchain to operate.
   iii. Oracles are used to deliver information to deterministic smart contracts.
   iv. The data from oracles improves the quality of decisions made by deterministic smart contracts.

a) ii only
b) i and iii
c) ii, iii and iv
d) All of the above

35. Which of the following is **false** about crypto currency wallets?
a) A wallet address is generated using a public key.
b) Options for storing private keys include hardware wallets.
c) A paper wallet is the most expensive option for storing private keys.
d) A hardware wallet is one example of offline storage for private keys.

36. Which of the following **least describes** barriers to adoption of Blockchain Technology?
a) Inability to influence other business network members
b) Costs of implementation
c) Regulatory uncertainty
d) Lack of knowledge and shortage of skilled personnel.

37. Which of the following **correctly describes** pre-image resistance?
a) Pre-image resistance implies that it possible that several different pre-images could result in the same digest.
b) Pre-image resistance implies that an input of any size to a hash function produces an output of a standard size.
c) Pre-image resistance implies that, even using computational brute force it is difficult to determine the pre-image from the resulting hash value.
d) Pre-image resistance implies that an input of any size to a hash function produces an output of a non-standard size.

38. Complete the following statement.
The frontend of a DApp is typically coded using tools like
____________________________.
a) Solidity, Vyper, Rust or Golang.
b) COBOL, ADA and Pascal
c) JavaScript, SCALA and R
d) Python, JavaScript, CSS and HTML.

39. Which of the following statements is **true** about the SSI Trust

Triangle?

a) It is used to represent the interaction among issuers, holders, and provers.
b) It is used to represent the interaction among issuers, holders, and verifiers.
c) It is used to represent the interaction among users, digital wallets, and DIDs.
d) It is used to represent the interaction among government, citizens, and regulators.

40. Complete the following statement.
To ensure non-repudiation, a sender signs his transactions using his own ____________ key.

a) private
b) public
c) consortium
d) group

41. Which of the following are **true** concerning digital signatures? (you may choose one or more)

i. The sender's private key is also referred to as the signing key.
ii. The signature verification component takes in as input, the transaction data, the sender's private key and digital signature.
iii. The sender's public key is also referred to as the signing key.
iv. The signature verification component takes in as input, the transaction data, the sender's public key and digital signature.

a) i only
b) i and iv
c) i, ii and iv
d) ii, iii and iv

42. Which of the following are **false** about SSI Wallets? (you may choose one or more)

i. Compared to edge wallets, the implementation of cloud wallets is lightweight and flexible.
ii. With edge wallets individuals must rely on a third-party provider to own, control, and manage their own wallet.

iii. SSI digital wallet should be implemented using open standards for portability of self-sovereign VCs and other sensitive private data.
iv. SSI wallets do not automatically maintain an encrypted backup of the data it manages.

a) i only
b) i and iii
c) ii and iv
d) All of the above

43. Which of the following are **not** acceptable examples of **Art NFTs**? (you may choose one or more)
i. Videos, 3D models, audios (music), books & prose.
ii. Collectibles, metaverse assets, trending memes and AI generated art.
iii. Enterprise NFTs.
iv. Virtual worlds on the internet like Decentraland and The Sandbox

a) i and ii
b) ii and iii
c) i, iii and iv
d) ii only

44. Which of the following industries is **most likely** to be attracted to blockchain due to its provenance tracking benefits?
a) Energy and utilities
b) Education
c) Supply chain
d) Medical

45. Which of the following statements **is not** a benefit of Blockchain-AI integration?
a) Decentralized training of AI models can help to preserve the privacy of the individual contributors.
b) AI's decisions cannot be audited since it uses cryptographic data for training.
c) Blockchain has the potential to improve the quality of data that AI trains on.
d) AI can improve blockchain's performance by predicting and managing transaction loads.

46. Which of the following statements is **false**?
  a) The tool used to view block information on a blockchain is called a block dashboard.
  b) Block height represents the number of blocks that have been confirmed in the entire history of a particular blockchain network.
  c) The block height at the genesis block is zero, because no blocks have been confirmed before it.
  d) A block explorer can be used to view block height of a particular block.

47. Which of the following are **true**? (you may choose one or more)
  i. On the Ethereum network, deployed contracts do not have addresses.
  ii. The contract deployment transaction is the transaction that sends the compiled code of a smart contract to the zero address to signify the registration of a new contract.
  iii. The zero address looks like "0x0000000000000000000000000000000000hhhhhh0".
  iv. The contract deployment transaction first executes on the local Ethereum node, and then propagates peer to peer, all over the network.
  a) i and iii
  b) ii and iii
  c) ii and iv
  d) None of the above

48. Complete the following statement.
When evaluating a blockchain solution and the benefits it could bring to a network of businesses, important concepts to consider are ________________________.
  a) Redundancy, Availability and Scalability
  b) Participants, Assets and Transactions
  c) Agile programming, Inheritance and Polymorphism
  d) Provenance, Immutability and Security

49. Fill in the blanks.
Bitcoin mining is an activity currently mostly carried out in mining farms using ______________, but can be carried out using ______________, albeit with much lower returns.

a) ASICs, CPU Rigs
b) GPU Rigs, CPU Rigs
c) CPU Rigs, ASICs
d) ASICs, GPU Rigs

50. Which of the following are **true**? (you may choose one or more)

i. A centralized application system is typically owned by various entities.
ii. Clients using a centralized application do not have to trust its owners.
iii. Clients using a centralized application have to trust its owners.
iv. For centralized applications, the server could be located either on the entity's own premises or with a cloud services provider

a) i and iv
b) ii and iii
c) i and iii
d) iii and iv

51. Which of the following is **true** regarding encryption mechanisms?

a) In asymmetric encryption, only one key is generated and is made private.
b) In symmetric encryption, a "man in the middle attack" occurs when the intended recipient colludes and forwards the message to adversaries of the sender.
c) In symmetric encryption a receiver does not require an inverse function to make the cipher message intelligible.
d) Public-private key pairs can be used to assure confidentiality.

52. Which of the following statements are **false**? (you may choose one or more)

i. Oracles are necessary for deterministic smart contracts to improve their quality of decision making.
ii. All consumers have the competence and the required knowledge to influence smart contract operations.
iii. Smart contracts are typically used in business transaction scenarios that target a large number of customers.

iv. In conformity with trustless systems, smart contracts, require trust between the parties, and external monitoring of contractual obligations or enforcement.

a) All except iii
b) ii and iv
c) i only
d) None of the above

53. Which of the following **best describes** a SSI digital agent?

a) This is a software module in the SSI infrastructure that operates digital wallets on behalf of the owner.
b) It either operates at the edge of the network, if it's an edge agent, or in the cloud if it is a cloud agent.
c) It is one of the building blocks of SSI.
d) It uses instructions from its owners, to communicate with other agents over the internet to form connections and exchange credentials.

54. When people are drawn to buy a cryptocurrency in anticipation that its value will rise and then they can sell it at a profit, we say the cryptocurrency has ________________________.

a) utility value
b) speculative value
c) altcoin use cases
d) rising value

55. Which of the following statements are **false** regarding NFTs? (you may choose one or more)

i. In terms of market valuation, it is enterprise NFTs that currently dominates, compared to NFTs from rare prestige art.
ii. Creating NFTs to represent trustworthy scientific papers can help in reducing plagiarism.
iii. NFTs cannot be used to facilitate fractional ownership of expensive assets such as real estate, aircrafts or yachts.
iv. NFTs can be used to represent official documents like national IDs.

a) i only
b) i and ii
c) i and iii
d) ii and iv

56. Which of the following is **not true** concerning the Ethereum network ?

a) The native cryptocurrency on the Ethereum blockchain network is called Ether.

b) The Ethereum network supports various applications beyond simple transfer of value.

c) Ethereum is a general purpose programmable blockchain.

d) Ethereum network was intended primarily for transferring ether (cryptocurrency) from one account to another.

57. Which of the following statements is **true** ?

a) Media and Entertainment industry is likely to be attracted to blockchain due to its disintermediation benefits.

b) The government is unlikely to be attracted to blockchain due to its identity management benefits.

c) There is no known use case for blockchain in the insurance industry.

d) The supply chain industry is most likely attracted to blockchain due to its user identity management benefits.

58. Fill in the blanks.

A blockchain bridge is a service that facilitates the movement of __________ and __________ between two different, otherwise isolated, ________________.

a) data, assets, sidechains

b) verifiable credentials, crypto, wallets

c) data, assets, blockchain networks

d) ones, zeros, blockchain networks

59. Which of the following statements is **false** ?

a) Some companies join consortium blockchain networks to accelerate learning and to influence standards.

b) A hard fork is a release of new software version that alters a blockchain system's functionality in a manner that is not backward compatible.

c) Distributed Ledger Technologies are a type of blockchain.

d) The allure to private-permissioned blockchains is that they provide assurances of resource efficiency, fast settlement times, confidentiality, and regulatory compliance.

60. Which of the following **disqualifies** blockchain as a potential solution? (you may choose one or more)
   i. Trusted third parties are desirable.
   ii. Same access rules exist for different participants.
   iii. High performance and low network latency are very critical requirements for business operations.
   iv. Only a single business participant is involved.
   a) i and ii only
   b) i and iv only
   c) i, iii and iv only
   d) All of the above

61. Which of the following statements regarding P2P sports betting are **true**? (you may choose one or more)
   i. It is more transparent than traditional sports betting.
   ii. Participants can bet for or against an event outcome.
   iii. There could be regulatory uncertainty due to the decentralized and international nature.
   iv. Bets might take some time before they are matched.
   a) i only
   b) i and iii
   c) i, ii and iv
   d) All of the above

62. Complete the following statement.
"Second pre-image resistance" is when ______________
   a) a hashing algorithm cannot infer the pre-image from the digest, even computationally, using brute force methods.
   b) a hashing algorithm cannot infer from the current input, a second pre-image that results in the same digest.
   c) two or more pre-images result in the same hash.
   d) a hashing algorithm can produce the pre-image from the digest, computationally, using brute force methods.

63. Which of the following is **false** regarding blockchain implementations?
   a) A blockchain system is applicable when high performance and low network latency are not critical

success factors.

b) A blockchain system is applicable when the transacting rules are likely to change.

c) A blockchain system is applicable when there is a need to share a database.

d) A blockchain system is applicable when trusted third parties are undesirable.

64. Which of the following is **true** regarding stablecoins ?

a) Stablecoin issuers maybe centralized, but they do not require auditing over the availability of advertised collateral.

b) Stablecoins are mostly used to facilitate trading across different cryptocurrency exchanges.

c) Stablecoins pegged 1:1 to a cryptocurrency are not likely to be subject to the price volatility of that cryptocurrency.

d) Most stablecoin issuers freely share their software source code and/or their APIs.

65. Which of the following statements **best** captures the impact of blockchain technologies in the Media and Entertainment industry?

a) Creators can receive more favorable income.

b) Creators can receive royalty payments directly.

c) Using smart contracts and NFTs, counterfeiting of digital products can be reduced.

d) Creators are enabled to interact directly with their customers or fans.

66. Which of the following statements are **false** regarding NFT standards in the Ethereum network? (you may choose one or more)

i. The NFT standard for identity claims is ERC-721.

ii. The general standard for NFTs is ERC-721.

iii. The general standard for NFTs is ERC-1155.

iv. The NFT standard for collectibles is ERC-721.

a) All are false

b) i and iii only

c) ii and iii only

d) i, iii and iv

67. Which of the following statements about SSI decentralized identifiers (DIDs) are **false**? (you may choose one or more)

i. DIDs make use of asymmetric-key cryptography.
ii. DIDs can be permanent and are meant to be machine readable.
iii. DIDs are similar to DNS names only to the extent that both are globally unique.
iv. DIDs are just like DNS names which are transferable and human readable.

a) i and iii
b) ii and iv
c) i, ii and iii
d) iv only

68. Which of the following statements are **true**? (you may choose one or more)

i. In solidity, smart contract code is organized in units similar to functions in OOP languages.
ii. In solidity, smart contracts methods are called procedures.
iii. In solidity, smart contract code is organized in units similar to classes in OOP languages.
iv. In solidity, smart contracts methods are called functions.

a) i only
b) ii only
c) i, ii and iii
d) iii and iv

69. Fill in the blanks.
A ____________ hosting the frontend of an Ethereum DApp can interact remotely with the DApp using the web3.js JavaScript library.

a) web server
b) blockchain
c) source code editor
d) plugin

70. Which of the following statements **least describe**s the benefits of blockchain networks?

a) Provenance, immutability and fault tolerance.
b) Efficiency, speed and elimination of middle men.
c) Cryptocurrencies and Decentralized Autonomous

Organizations.
d) Censorship resistance.

71. Which of the following statements is **false**?
a) Blockchain technology is heavily dependent on cryptography.
b) Quantum resistance refers to cryptographic algorithms and systems that are not vulnerable to attacks using quantum computers.
c) In the pre-quantum era, security for current blockchain systems could be compromised.
d) Quantum computers are expected to be much faster than contemporary computers.

72. Which of the following statements is **true**?
a) Transactions sent to smart contract addresses may contain only data as parameters.
b) Decentralized Autonomous Organizations are special kinds of smart contacts.
c) Ethereum smart contracts are written in EVM bytecode using Solidity.
d) Smart contract generated transactions cannot change the state of the blockchain.

73. Fill in the blanks.
____________________ uses ring signatures as a solution to the privacy problem.
a) RippleNet
b) Monero
c) Bitcoin
d) Ethereum

74. Which of the following is **false** about SSI Governance frameworks?
a) Governance frameworks is a set of business, legal, and technical rules created and administered by an entity known as the governance authority.
b) Governance frameworks specify only what a governance authority can or cannot do.
c) Governance frameworks guide issuers on the policies and procedures that must be followed to issue a credential.

d) Governance frameworks may specify the terms and conditions to which verifiers must agree to verify credentials and/or, the terms and conditions to which holders must agree to obtain credentials.

75. Which of the following describes the property of "Completeness" in Zero Knowledge Proof Systems?
   a) If the statement is false, every dishonest party (prover) can convince honest verifiers.
   b) If the statement is true, no verifying party can learn anything besides the fact that the statement is true.
   c) If the statement is false, no dishonest party (prover) can convince honest verifiers.
   d) If the statement is true, an honest verifying party will be convinced by an honest prover.

76. Which of the following are **true**? (you may choose one or more)
   i. A program known as Vyper is required so that a DApp can receive information external to its native blockchain network.
   ii. By design, DApps cannot work with resources within the blockchain network due to technical and trust issues.
   iii. Conceptually, an Oracle is like a bridge between a blockchain and the world outside the blockchain.
   iv. By design, DApps only work with resources within the blockchain network due to technical and trust issues.
   a) i only
   b) i and ii
   c) ii and iii
   d) iii and iv

77. Blockchain technology's decentralized nature makes it ________________.
   a) tamper resistant
   b) immutable
   c) encrypt-able
   d) fault tolerant

78. Which of the following statements are **false**? (you may choose one or more)

i. Blockchain systems are not outright replacements for traditional databases.
ii. To determine relevance or usefulness of blockchains in a given industry, we must put into consideration the asset(s) to be tokenized.
iii. A blockchain system implementation is applicable, if an objective immutable log is not required.
iv. Blockchain system implementations only make sense where there is a network of collaborating parties whose transactions evolve around a shared set of assets in the network.

a) iii only
b) ii and iii
c) i, ii and iv
d) None of the above

79. Which of the following **least describes** security tokens?
a) Security tokens can be used to represent physical or digital assets.
b) Security tokens are digital assets whose ownership is recorded on a blockchain.
c) Security tokens are recorded on a distributed ledger.
d) Security tokens can facilitate fractional ownership of assets and thus increase liquidity in traditionally illiquid markets.

80. Which of the following is an **unlikely** blockchain technology use case in the government sector?
a) P2P Betting
b) Accountability
c) Research
d) Efficiency

81. Which of the following statements is **false**?
a) Token standards are like templates or blueprints that can be used to guide development.
b) An NFT is a physical asset whose ownership is recorded on a blockchain.
c) Different blockchain networks are likely to have their own token standards.
d) Tokens that are used to represent ownership are like

certificates of authenticity.

82. Which of the following **best describes** an advantage of smart contracts?
   a) Smart contracts lower the risk of collaboration because their functionality is transparent, predictable, and independently verifiable by scrutinizing the source code.
   b) Smart contracts preempt the possibility of disappointment.
   c) Smart contracts are trustless systems.
   d) Smart contracts can be used for creating DAOs.

83. Which of the following statements is **true**?
   a) Blockchain technology can be used to track consumption and payments in a decentralized energy production ecosystem.
   b) The education sector has no other use for blockchain technology, apart from identity management.
   c) There is completely no use case for blockchain in the energy and utilities sector.
   d) Blockchain technology is the best tool to help the government subvert voting processes.

84. Fill in the blanks.
   A sidechain is connected to its ___________ using a ___________.
   a) parent, oracles
   b) child network, two-way peg
   c) oracles, parent network
   d) mainnet, two-way peg

85. Which of the following statements about SSI features/benefits are **false**? (you may choose one or more)
   i. Using guardianship credentials, an entity can operate SSI agents and wallets on behalf of another entity.
   ii. An SSI user agent can make a digitally signed request to other agents for erasure of personal data and later verify if the request was honored.
   iii. Using SSI workflow automation, it is possible to achieve a worldwide Business Process Automation (BPA).
   iv. A guardianship credential is exactly the same as a

delegation credential.

a) iii only
b) i, ii and iii
c) iv only
d) None of the above

86. Which of the following statements is **false**?

a) Cryptocurrency wallets are decentralized applications.
b) Use cases for DApps increased after the launch of Ethereum.
c) DApps can only be created to run on general purpose programmable blockchains.
d) DApps are replicated on each node of a blockchain network.

87. Which of the following **is true** regarding the substitution method of encryption? (you may choose one or more)

i. The encryption method is so simple that by repeated guesswork alone, even without a computer, one could infer the actual message from the cipher text.
ii. The encryption/decryption mechanism has to be kept secret.
iii. Once an entity has known the encryption/decryption method, they could intercept a message, decrypt, modify it, encrypt it again and send it on its way.
iv. The encryption/decryption mechanism does not have to be kept secret.

a) iv only
b) iii only
c) i, ii, and iii
d) All of the above

88. Which of the following statement is **true** about ICOs?

a) Prior to an ICO, the concerned startup is required to register with a government regulatory agency.
b) After an ICO, a startup is required to provide financial statements as well as business updates to the public investors.
c) Prior to an ICO, startup founders are subjected to thorough background checks.
d) Coins issued at an ICO are traded at cryptocurrency

exchanges, which are not all subject to regulation.

89. Fill in the blanks.
_____________________ is the ability of a blockchain network to resist attempts to censor, alter, or stop the flow of information.
a) Provenance
b) Censorship resistance
c) Censorship disabled
d) Immutability

90. Complete the sentence.
The implementation of blockchain technology would be unnecessary or even detrimental for ____.
a) basic food service, Supply chain and Oil & Gas
b) manual labor services, traditional hairdressing and, small-scale agriculture with local customers
c) Education, Healthcare and Real Estate
d) Supply chain, Real estate, and Education

91. Which of the following statements is **true**?
a) A distributed application system presents itself to clients like multiple systems, even though it is installed on just one single central server.
b) A distributed application system is a trustless system.
c) A distributed application system is typically under the authority of one entity.
d) A distributed application system is only found on blockchain networks.

92. Which of the following statements are **true** regarding smart contract shortcomings? (you may choose one or more)
i. Smart contracts eliminate the possibility of legal disputes.
ii. Smart contracts are on the verge of replacing contract law.
iii. Smart contracts are unable to give any consideration to new developments that its designers/programmers had not taken into account.
iv. Only a small subset of users might be in a position to truly understand a smart contract's code in order to verify its functionality.

a) i only
b) iii only
c) i and iv
d) iii and iv

93. Which of the following statements represent citizens' fears on what the government might end up doing after implementation of CBDCs? (You may choose more than one)

i. To punish dissent.
ii. To totally control their citizens finances and assets, and consequently, to control their behavior.
iii. To facilitate surveillance capitalism.
iv. To enforce unpopular mandates such as vaccinations.

a) ii only
b) iii only
c) iv only
d) All of the above

94. Which of the following **least describes** a blockchain fork?

a) A blockchain fork occurs when the blockchain splits into two competing paths.
b) A blockchain fork occurs when the unwilling nodes on the network are under no obligation to upgrade to a backward incompatible protocol, but can still use it.
c) A blockchain fork occurs when there is an update on the consensus mechanism of the blockchain.
d) In a blockchain fork, a permanent split is created between the new and the old blockchain, resulting in two separate blockchains, both operating concurrently.

95. Fill in the blanks.
Unlike in ICOs where price is determined by the __________, IDO prices are determined by ____________ on the DEX.

a) regulators, market dynamics
b) dollar demand, regulators
c) issuer, market dynamics
d) issuer, price of bitcoin

96. Which of the following **best describes** the use of blockchain technology in the education sector?

a) Record keeping, claims verification, payouts

b) Record keeping, verification of credentials, identity management
c) Consumption tracking, voting, finality
d) Micro payments tracking, claims verification, payouts

97. Fill in the blanks.
A ______________________ is a data structure representing a large amount of data that has compressed into a single hash and can be queried for the presence of specific components in the data.
a) hash tree
b) hash collision
c) leaf hash
d) root path

98. Three of the following blockchain platforms are purpose-built for SSI. Which one is not?
a) Ethereum
b) Hyperledger Indy
c) Veres One
d) Sovrin Network

99. Complete the following statement.
All of the following are non-fungible except ____________.
a) Fiat currencies
b) Digital collectibles
c) Video game items
d) Tokenized physical assets

100. Fill in the blanks.
We end up with a ________________________, if the public have access to the system and transactions are transparent to the public.
a) public permission-less blockchain
b) private permission-less blockchain
c) private permissioned blockchain
d) public permissioned blockchain

Answers to Quizzes

"On two occasions I have been asked, 'Pray, Mr. Babbage, if you put into the machine wrong figures, will the right answers come out?' I am not able rightly to apprehend the kind of confusion of ideas that could provoke such a question."
- Charles Babbage

Quiz 1

1. **D**	2. **C**	3. **A**	4. **D**	5. **B**
6. **B**	7. **C**	8. **C**	9. **D**	10. **A**

Quiz 2

1. **C**	2. **A**	3. **D**	4. **B**	5. **B**
6. **A**	7. **C**	8. **C**	9. **C**	10. **A**

Quiz 3

1. **D**	2. **A**	3. **A**	4. **B**	5. **C**
6. **C**	7. **D**	8. **C**	9. **B**	10. **B**

Quiz 4

1. **D**	2. **C**	3. **C**	4. **A**	5. **B**
6. **B**	7. **A**	8. **D**	9. **C**	10. **A**

Quiz 5

1. **C**	2. **A**	3. **A**	4. **B**	5. **D**
6. **C**	7. **C**	8. **C**	9. **C**	10. **B**

Quiz 6

1. **D**	2. **C**	3. **A**	4. **A**	5. **C**
6. **B**	7. **B**	8. **C**	9. **D**	10. **A**

Quiz 7

1.	**A**	2.	**B**	3.	**C**	4.	**C**	5.	**C**
6.	**D**	7.	**B**	8.	**A**	9.	**A**	10.	**D**

Quiz 8

1.	**D**	2.	**C**	3.	**C**	4.	**A**	5.	**B**
6.	**D**	7.	**A**	8.	**A**	9.	**B**	10.	**C**

Quiz 9

1.	**C**	2.	**D**	3.	**A**	4.	**C**	5.	**B**
6.	**A**	7.	**D**	8.	**B**	9.	**C**	10.	**C**

Quiz 10

1.	**B**	2.	**D**	3.	**D**	4.	**C**	5.	**B**
6.	**A**	7.	**A**	8.	**A**	9.	**D**	10.	**C**

Answers to Exams

"Like all young men I set out to be a genius, but mercifully laughter intervened"

- Clea Lawrence Durrell

Exam 1

1.	**D**	21.	**A**	41.	**D**	61.	**D**	81.	**D**
2.	**C**	22.	**D**	42.	**A**	62.	**D**	82.	**A**
3.	**A**	23.	**C**	43.	**D**	63.	**B**	83.	**D**
4.	**D**	24.	**C**	44.	**B**	64.	**C**	84.	**B**
5.	**A**	25.	**D**	45.	**C**	65.	**A**	85.	**B**
6.	**C**	26.	**C**	46.	**C**	66.	**A**	86.	**C**
7.	**B**	27.	**B**	47.	**C**	67.	**C**	87.	**A**
8.	**A**	28.	**D**	48.	**B**	68.	**D**	88.	**D**
9.	**D**	29.	**D**	49.	**A**	69.	**B**	89.	**B**
10.	**B**	30.	**D**	50.	**A**	70.	**B**	90.	**C**
11.	**C**	31.	**B**	51.	**D**	71.	**B**	91.	**B**
12.	**B**	32.	**C**	52.	**A**	72.	**D**	92.	**C**
13.	**A**	33.	**D**	53.	**B**	73.	**A**	93.	**A**
14.	**B**	34.	**A**	54.	**C**	74.	**C**	94.	**A**
15.	**B**	35.	**C**	55.	**C**	75.	**D**	95.	**A**
16.	**B**	36.	**C**	56.	**D**	76.	**C**	96.	**C**
17.	**C**	37.	**D**	57.	**B**	77.	**B**	97.	**D**
18.	**C**	38.	**A**	58.	**A**	78.	**D**	98.	**A**
19.	**D**	39.	**A**	59.	**C**	79.	**A**	99.	**D**
20.	**A**	40.	**B**	60.	**D**	80.	**D**	100.	**D**

Exam 2

"Failure is simply the opportunity to begin again, this time more intelligently."
— Henry Ford

1.	**B**	21.	**A**	41.	**B**	61.	**D**	81.	**B**
2.	**C**	22.	**A**	42.	**C**	62.	**B**	82.	**A**
3.	**A**	23.	**C**	43.	**C**	63.	**B**	83.	**A**
4.	**B**	24.	**C**	44.	**C**	64.	**B**	84.	**D**
5.	**A**	25.	**C**	45.	**B**	65.	**A**	85.	**C**
6.	**D**	26.	**B**	46.	**A**	66.	**D**	86.	**C**
7.	**B**	27.	**D**	47.	**C**	67.	**D**	87.	**C**
8.	**C**	28.	**D**	48.	**B**	68.	**D**	88.	**D**
9.	**D**	29.	**D**	49.	**D**	69.	**A**	89.	**B**
10.	**C**	30.	**B**	50.	**D**	70.	**C**	90.	**B**
11.	**C**	31.	**C**	51.	**D**	71.	**C**	91.	**C**
12.	**D**	32.	**B**	52.	**A**	72.	**B**	92.	**D**
13.	**D**	33.	**C**	53.	**A**	73.	**B**	93.	**D**
14.	**A**	34.	**D**	54.	**B**	74.	**B**	94.	**B**
15.	**C**	35.	**C**	55.	**C**	75.	**D**	95.	**C**
16.	**B**	36.	**A**	56.	**D**	76.	**D**	96.	**B**
17.	**B**	37.	**C**	57.	**A**	77.	**D**	97.	**A**
18.	**B**	38.	**D**	58.	**C**	78.	**A**	98.	**A**
19.	**D**	39.	**B**	59.	**C**	79.	**C**	99.	**A**
20.	**C**	40.	**A**	60.	**D**	80.	**A**	100.	**A**

Recommended Readings

"If I have seen further than others, it is by standing on the shoulders of Giants"
– Isaac Newton

The following list comprises of some books on blockchain technology that you might enjoy reading.

1. Self-Sovereign Identity: Decentralized digital identity and verifiable credentials by Alex Preukschat, Drummond Reed.
2. Blockchain Fundamentals for Web 3.0 by Mary C. Lacity & Steven C. Lupien
3. Cryptoassets : The Innovative Investor's Guide to Bitcoin and Beyond by Chris Burniske and Jack Tatar
4. Security Tokens and Stablecoins: Quick Start Guide – by Weimin Sun, Xun (Brian) Wu and Angela Kwok
5. Solidity Programming Essentials by Ritesh Modi
6. Building Ethereum Dapps: Decentralized Applications on the Ethereum Blockchain by Robert Infante.
7. Mastering Bitcoin Unlocking Digital Cryptocurrencies by Andreas M. Antonopoulos
8. The NFT Handbook How to Create, Sell and Buy Non-Fungible Tokens by Matt Fortnow and QuHarrison Terry
9. Blockchain Democracy Technology, Law and the Rule of the Crowd by William Magnuson
10. Build Your Own Blockchain A Practical Guide to Distributed Ledger Technology by Daniel Hellwig, Goran Karlic, & Arnd Huchzermeier

Disclaimer

This book is strictly for knowledge/education purposes. Nothing contained herein shall constitute a solicitation, recommendation, endorsement, or offer by Edwin S. Ongola to invest in Cryptocurrencies, NFTs or any Blockchain project.

Made in the USA
Monee, IL
04 November 2026

67374650R00164